THE EGGHEADS QUIZ BOOK

THE EGGHEADS QUIZ BOOK

CORGI BOOKS

TRANSWORLD PUBLISHERS
61-63 Uxbridge Road, London W5 5SA
A Random House Group Company
www.rbooks.co.uk
THE EGGHEADS QUIZ BOOK
A CORGI BOOK: 9780552156783

First publication in Great Britain
Corgi edition published 2007

Published in association with the 12 Yard Productions
television series Eggheads

A CIP catalogue record for this book
is available from the British Library.

Addresses for Random House Group Ltd companies outside the UK
can be found at: www.randomhouse.co.uk
The Random House Group Ltd Reg. No. 954009

The Random House Group Ltd makes every effort to ensure that
the papers used in its books are made from trees that have been
legally sourced from well-managed and credibly certified forests.
Our paper procurement policy can be found at:
www.randomhouse.co.uk/paper.htm

Typeset in Stone by
Falcon Oast Graphic Art Ltd.

Printed in the UK by CPI Cox & Wyman, Reading, RG1 8EX.

2 4 6 8 10 9 7 5 3 1

Contents

Acknowledgements

We would like to take this opportunity to thank some of the people who have contributed to the success of *Eggheads* over the years.

Dermot Murnaghan for making the show his own.

The Eggheads themselves: Kevin Ashman, C. J. De Mooi, Daphne Fowler, Chris Hughes and Judith Keppel, for their knowledge and dogged resolution to defeat all-comers and defend their reputation.

Everyone at the BBC who has been supportive of the show, with special thanks to Alison Sharman, Gilly Hall, Jay Hunt, Roly Keating and Sumi Connock.

Thanks to the all of the production teams and crew who have worked so hard on the show over the years – in particular Nick Pagan and his team for writing the thousands of questions used across the series.

To the talented people who have produced the show: Rob Dean, Tessa McHugh, Andrew Musson and Eileen Herlihy.

To Joanna Kaye at KBJ Management and to Amanda Preston at Luigi Bonomi Associates.

Our special thanks to all the teams who have attempted to defeat the Eggheads despite the obvious difficulties this task entails.

And, finally, our thanks to the viewers for their attention and loyalty. We hope that you continue to enjoy the show.

David Young and Andy Culpin
Executive Producers

Introduction

Hello and welcome to *The Eggheads Quiz Book*. You've seen them on TV, and now you have the chance to test your knowledge against the most formidable quiz team in the country.

Since 2003, I have been quizmaster to Chris, Daphne, C. J., Kevin and Judith as they have taken on all-comers, and still they amaze me. Whether it's Chris giving us an impromptu lecture on the British army's retreat from Kabul in 1842, Daphne surprising us with her knowledge of dance-music duo The Chemical Brothers, or Kevin knowing so much he has been nicknamed 'The Human Google', you begin to wonder if the Eggheads can ever be beaten.

But it has happened.

Students have beaten them, civil servants have beaten them and helicopter pilots have beaten them. In one amazing result, a team of postmen from the Isle of Lewis beat them.

So, can you replicate these successes and defeat Britain's brainiest boffins?

I hope you enjoy the book.

Dermot Murnaghan

JUDITH KEPPEL Arts & Books

Full name:
Judith Keppel

Home town:
Born in Shropshire, Judith now lives in France and London.

Education:
Her father was in the armed services, so Judith went to eight different schools around England including St Mary's School in Wantage where she was a boarder, and a convent school in Malta. Judith also has a degree in History of Art and History from UCL.

Quizzing credentials:
In 2000, Judith became the first person to win £1 million on *Who Wants to Be a Millionaire?*

Strongest Eggheads subject:
Arts and Books

Least favourite subject:
Sport

Special interest:
English literature, gardening and renovating her house in France.

Arts & Books

1. Which artist famously cut off part of his own ear after an altercation with his friend Paul Gauguin?

O Vincent Van Gogh

O Claude Monet

O Henri de Toulouse-Lautrec

2. The artist Roy Lichtenstein is most commonly associated with which artistic movement?

O Impressionism

O Surrealism

O Pop Art

3. *Captain Corelli's Mandolin* is a bestselling novel by which author?

O Louis de Bernières

O Nick Hornby

O Dan Brown

4. Which Shakespeare play features three witches, collectively known as the Weird Sisters?

O *Macbeth*

O *Hamlet*

O *Othello*

5. What is the name of the central character in the Truman Capote novella *Breakfast at Tiffany's*?

O Holly Golightly

O Sugar Kane

O Rose Sayer

6. *The Female Eunuch* is an influential 1970 book by which author?

O Andrea Dworkin

O Germaine Greer

O Simone de Beauvoir

7. Which British artist is famous for the *Natural History* series featuring the bodies of animals preserved in formaldehyde?

- O Damien Hirst
- O Tracey Emin
- O Steve McQueen

8. *The Four Seasons* is an eighteenth-century work by which composer?

- O Mozart
- O Schubert
- O Vivaldi

9. *Arms and the Man* is a play by which author?

- O Noël Coward
- O Henry Miller
- O George Bernard Shaw

10. In J. K. Rowling's Harry Potter novels, what is the name of the Ravenclaw girl who has a brief romance with Harry?

- O Dolores Umbridge
- O Cho Chang
- O Bellatrix Lestrange

11. What is the name of the narrator of the J. D. Salinger book *The Catcher in the Rye*?

- O Holden Caulfield
- O Scout Finch
- O Sean Bateman

12. Which writer created the fictional fighter pilot Biggles?

- O P. C. Wren
- O Sapper
- O W. E. Johns

13. Which Arthur Miller play is based on the true story of the seventeenth-century Salem witch trials?

O *The Crucible*

O *Death of a Salesman*

O *All My Sons*

14. Which German town is the site of an annual festival celebrating the music of the composer Richard Wagner?

O Bonn

O Dresden

O Bayreuth

15. What is the title of the controversial 1987 book written by the former MI5 operative Peter Wright?

O *The Fifth Man*

O *Undercover*

O *Spycatcher*

16. *The Thirty-Nine Steps* is an adventure story by which writer?

O H. Rider Haggard

O John Buchan

O C. S. Forester

17. Which French artist is famous for his series of water lily paintings?

O Delacroix

O Toulouse-Lautrec

O Monet

18. Who is the 'Prisoner of Azkaban' in the third book of J. K. Rowling's Harry Potter series?

O Remus Lupin

O Sirius Black

O Peter Pettigrew

19. The stage play *Amadeus* depicts the life of which composer?

- O Mozart
- O Chopin
- O Tchaikovsky

20. 'Anthem for Doomed Youth' is a poem by which author?

- O Stephen Spender
- O Wilfred Owen
- O Ezra Pound

21. In which city was the painter L. S. Lowry born?

- O Manchester
- O Liverpool
- O Leeds

22. With which branch of the arts is Barbara Hepworth most closely associated?

- O Ballet
- O Sculpture
- O Poetry

23. What is the name of the title character in the Thackeray novel *Vanity Fair*?

- O Becky Sharp
- O Bathsheba Everdene
- O Helen Graham

24. Which twentieth-century poet wrote the lines: 'Do not go gentle into that good night. Rage, rage against the dying of the light'?

- O Ted Hughes
- O T. S. Eliot
- O Dylan Thomas

25. Which Puccini opera is set amongst the poor writers and artists of nineteenth-century Paris?

- O *Madame Butterfly*
- O *Turandot*
- O *La Bohème*

26. In J. M. Barrie's *Peter Pan*, what type of dog is Nana?

- O Irish Wolfhound
- O Doberman
- O Newfoundland

27. 'The Raven' is a famous poem by which American writer?

- O Edgar Allan Poe
- O Robert Frost
- O Allen Ginsberg

28. What was the name of the heroic workhorse in George Orwell's allegorical novel *Animal Farm*?

- O Snowball
- O Boxer
- O Benjamin

29. Which 1928 play by R. C. Sherriff is set in the trenches of the First World War?

- O *Journey's End*
- O *Windfall*
- O *Badger's Green*

30. In which branch of the arts was Antonio Gaudi a leading figure of the twentieth century?

- O Ballet
- O Architecture
- O Poetry

31. The nineteenth-century poet Alfred, Lord Tennyson wrote a celebrated poem about which famous military action?

- O The Charge of the Light Brigade
- O The Battle of Waterloo
- O The Siege of Mafeking

32. In which fictional country was the 1894 adventure novel *The Prisoner of Zenda* set?

- O Latveria
- O Arcadia
- O Ruritania

33. *The Dance of the Sugar Plum Fairy* is a piece of music by which composer?

- O Tchaikovsky
- O Beethoven
- O Berlioz

34. The artist Salvador Dalí was born in which country?

- O Spain
- O Italy
- O Germany

35. *Paradise Lost* is a seventeenth-century poem by which author?

- O John Milton
- O Ben Jonson
- O John Donne

36. The *Moonlight Sonata* is a work by which composer?

- O Beethoven
- O Mozart
- O Chopin

37. In 1755, which writer published his *Dictionary of the English Language*?

O Samuel Johnson

O James Boswell

O Jonathan Swift

38. In which field of the arts are Gilbert and George leading names?

O Architecture

O Modern art

O Ballet

39. What is the name of the despicable bully who tortures the title character in the popular novel *Tom Brown's Schooldays*?

O Flashman

O East

O Arnold

40. Sebastian Flyte and Charles Ryder are characters in which book?

O *Brideshead Revisited*

O *Another Country*

O *Goodbye, Mr Chips*

41. *The Hallelujah Chorus* is a piece of music by which composer?

O Brahms

O Stravinsky

O Handel

42. In *The Hitchhikers' Guide to the Galaxy*, what number is the answer to life, the universe and everything?

O Thirty-two

O Forty-two

O Fifty-two

43. In ballet, 'sissone' and 'soubresaut' are examples of what type of movement?

- Jump
- Lift
- Bend

44. *Carmina Burana*, as famously featured in the Old Spice TV advertisements, is a choral work by which composer?

- Bach
- Orff
- Offenbach

45. The *Enigma Variations* is a nineteenth-century work by which composer?

- Holst
- Elgar
- Delius

46. In which of Shakespeare's plays does the phrase 'brave new world' appear?

- *The Tempest*
- *Hamlet*
- *The Winter's Tale*

47. 'He was a sympathiser to the poor, the suffering, and the oppressed; and by his death, one of England's greatest writers is lost to the world', is an inscription of the tomb of which writer?

- Geoffrey Chaucer
- Charles Dickens
- William Shakespeare

48. Which bestselling book of 1969 was written by Mario Puzo?

- *The Exorcist*
- *Jaws*
- *The Godfather*

49. *The Beach* is a novel by which author?

- O Alex Garland
- O Stel Pavlou
- O Andy McNab

50. Who was the Poet Laureate between 1967 and 1972?

- O Cecil Day-Lewis
- O Ted Hughes
- O John Betjeman

51. The artist John Constable is most closely associated with which part of the UK?

- O Scottish Highlands
- O East Anglia
- O Welsh Valleys

52. What is the name of the central character in the Dan Brown novels *Angels and Demons* and *The Da Vinci Code*?

- O Robert Langdon
- O Dirk Pitt
- O Bernard Samson

53. 'Ozymandias' is a famous poem by which writer?

- O John Keats
- O Percy Bysshe Shelley
- O William Wordsworth

54. What name is given to a work of art that has been painted on wet plaster?

- O Fresco
- O Triptych
- O Icon

55. Which French artist created the 1872 painting *Impression: Sunrise* from which Impressionism takes its name?

- O Monet
- O Manet
- O Pissarro

56. Which ballet dancer, born in Riga in 1948, defected from the Soviet Union during a 1974 tour to North America?

- O Mikhail Baryshnikov
- O Rudolf Nureyev
- O Vaslav Nijinsky

57. *Carmen* is an 1875 opera by which composer?

- O Bizet
- O Puccini
- O Verdi

58. Who is the central character in John Osborne's 1956 play *Look Back in Anger*?

- O Willy Loman
- O Jimmy Porter
- O Archie Rice

59. What was the first name of the British poet Lord Byron?

- O George
- O James
- O Timothy

60. Ann-Sophie Mutter is a virtuoso performer on which musical instrument?

- O Violin
- O Clarinet
- O Piano

61. Whose last words are reputed to be, 'My wallpaper and I are fighting a battle to the death. One or the other of us has to go'?

- Winston Churchill
- Oscar Wilde
- Dorothy Parker

62. Which story by Rudyard Kipling tells the story of the British adventurers Daniel Dravot and Peachey Carnehan?

- The Man Who Would Be King
- The Light that Failed
- Gunga Din

63. The villainous Mrs Danvers is a character in which novel?

- *Gone with the Wind*
- *Rebecca*
- *East of Eden*

64. 'The Secret Life of Walter Mitty' is a short story by which writer?

- James Thurber
- Dorothy Parker
- F. Scott Fitzgerald

65. What is the name of the only novel to feature Dashiell Hammett's hard-boiled private eye, Sam Spade?

- *The Long Goodbye*
- *Out of the Past*
- *The Maltese Falcon*

66. *Rosencrantz and Guildenstern Are Dead* is an award-winning play by which writer?

- Alan Bennett
- Harold Pinter
- Tom Stoppard

67. Philip Larkin became the librarian of which university in 1955?

- O Hull
- O Brunel
- O UEA

68. What is the title of the only opera to be written by Ludwig Van Beethoven?

- O *Fidelio*
- O *Lotario*
- O *Oreste*

69. In the David Hockney painting *Mr and Mrs Clark and Percy*, what is Percy?

- O Budgie
- O Dog
- O Cat

70. What is the first name of Bernard Cornwell's fictional soldier Sharpe?

- O Raymond
- O Robert
- O Richard

71. Dolores Haze is a major character in which twentieth-century novel?

- O *Catch-22*
- O *Lolita*
- O *Tender Is the Night*

72. Which British novelist sometimes worked under the pseudonym of Boz?

- O Charles Dickens
- O William Makepeace Thackeray
- O Henry Fielding

73. Which play by David Mamet features a group of desperate real estate salesmen?

- O *American Buffalo*
- O *Oleanna*
- O *Glengarry Glen Ross*

74. The central character in Mark Haddon's book *The Curious Incident of the Dog in the Night-Time* suffers from which medical condition?

- O Asperger's
- O Bipolar Disorder
- O Tourette's

75. Which writer created the fictional character Simon Templar, also known as The Saint?

- O Baroness Orczy
- O Leslie Charteris
- O Georges Simenon

76. 'He was my north, my south, my east and west, my working week and my Sunday rest,' taken from 'Funeral Blues', is a quotation from which writer?

- O W. H. Auden
- O Stephen Spender
- O T. S. Eliot

77. What was the name of the friend and regular travelling companion of the fictional detective Hercule Poirot?

- O Thomas Beresford
- O Inspector Lestrade
- O Arthur Hastings

78. What is the name of the title character in J. R. R. Tolkien's *Lord of the Rings* trilogy?

- O Saruman
- O Wormtongue
- O Sauron

79. The trilby hat takes its name from the title of a work by which writer?

- *O* George du Maurier
- *O* Henry James
- *O* Edith Wharton

80. Who famously described Lord Byron as, 'mad, bad and dangerous to know'?

- *O* Lady Caroline Lamb
- *O* Daisy Brooke
- *O* Lady Emma Hamilton

81. Which writer won the 2001 Booker Prize for *The True History of the Kelly Gang*?

- *O* Ian McEwan
- *O* Michael Ondaatje
- *O* Peter Carey

82. Which opera by Giuseppe Verdi features a humpbacked jester in the title role?

- *O* *La Traviata*
- *O* *Aida*
- *O* *Rigoletto*

83. *The Fighting Temeraire, Tugged to Her Last Berth to Be Broken Up* is one of the most famous works of which artist?

- *O* Lowry
- *O* Constable
- *O* Turner

84. The musician Daniel Barenboim is best known for his skill on which musical instrument?

- *O* Piano
- *O* Violin
- *O* Cello

85. Who did the writer Marlowe refer to as, 'The face that launched a thousand ships'?

- O Helen of Troy
- O Elizabeth I
- O Cleopatra

86. By the start of the nineteenth century, Ludwig Van Beethoven was beginning to suffer from which condition?

- O Blindness
- O Muteness
- O Deafness

87. *Rosemary's Baby* and *The Boys from Brazil* are books by which author?

- O Ira Levin
- O Arthur Hailey
- O James Michener

88. Which artist, born in the fifteenth century, gave his name to a shade of brownish orange – a colour that featured heavily in his artwork?

- O Titian
- O Canaletto
- O Giotto

89. What was the name of Mozart's father?

- O Leonard
- O Leopold
- O Ludwig

90. What is the name of the central character in Patrick O'Brien's historical novel *Master and Commander*?

- O Thomas Cochrane
- O Jack Aubrey
- O John Charity Spring

91. With which type of theatrical work is the writer and director Ray Cooney most commonly associated?

- O Ballet
- O Musicals
- O Farce

92. What is the name of the central character in Philip Pullman's *His Dark Materials* trilogy?

- O Lyra
- O Caspian
- O Lysander

93. *The Night Watch* and *The Jewish Bride* are paintings by which artist?

- O Rembrandt
- O Rubens
- O Van Dyck

94. Who has written a series of crime novels featuring Dr Kay Scarpetta?

- O P. J. Tracy
- O Harlan Coben
- O Patricia Cornwell

95. What type of musical instrument is a 'flageolet'?

- O Drum
- O Flute
- O Clarinet

96. Who is the villain in Shakespeare's tragedy *Othello*?

- O Edgar
- O Iago
- O Don John

97. What was the name of the Madison Avenue studio used by the artist Andy Warhol and his entourage?

- O The Warehouse
- O The Factory
- O The Workshop

98. Which famous novel starts with the line: 'It was a bright, cold day in April and the clocks were striking thirteen'?

- O *A Clockwork Orange*
- O *1984*
- O *Brave New World*

99. Which artist, born in January 1912, was nicknamed 'Jack the Dripper', because of his unusual painting style?

- O Jackson Pollock
- O Jack Vettriano
- O Jack Coggins

100. Which musical work of the twentieth century is set in Catfish Row?

- O *Porgy and Bess*
- O *Carmen Jones*
- O *Anything Goes*

101. In which adventure story does Blind Pew give the Black Spot to Billy Bones?

- O *Kidnapped!*
- O *Ivanhoe*
- O *Treasure Island*

102. What is the first name of the title character in the 1925 novel *The Great Gatsby*?

- O Jerome
- O Jay
- O Joshua

103. What is the name of the helicopter featured in the title of several children's books written by Sarah Ferguson, the Duchess of York?

- O Budgie
- O Torchy
- O Towelly

104. Which children's book of 1863 was written by Charles Kingsley?

- O *The Water Babies*
- O *Doctor Dolittle*
- O *Black Beauty*

105. 'Hope springs eternal in the human breast,' is a line first penned by which writer?

- O Alexander Pope
- O John Keats
- O Thomas Hardy

106. *Pomp and Circumstance* is a series of five marches by which British composer?

- O Elgar
- O Bax
- O Purcell

107. 'I will show you fear in a handful of dust,' is a line first written by which American-born poet?

- O Emily Dickinson
- O Robert Frost
- O T. S. Eliot

108. In the tales by Beatrix Potter what was Miss Moppet?

- O Cat
- O Goose
- O Fox

109. 'Oh, my love's like a red, red rose,' is a famous line written by which poet?

- O William Shakespeare
- O Dylan Thomas
- O Robert Burns

110. The artist Paul Gauguin left France to live on which island in 1891?

- O Tahiti
- O Hawaii
- O Fiji

111. Which member of the Beatles released a 1997 symphonic work entitled *Standing Stone*?

- O George Harrison
- O Paul McCartney
- O Ringo Starr

112. Johann Sebastian Bach's *Tocatta e Fugue in D Minor* is a composition for which musical instrument?

- O Cello
- O Piano
- O Organ

113. In classical literature, *Lives of the Caesars* was an influential work by which Roman writer?

- O Cato
- O Suetonius
- O Horace

114. Which English playwright, rumoured to be a government agent, died in a bar room brawl in 1593?

- O Christopher Marlowe
- O Ben Jonson
- O John Fletcher

115. Starbuck and Ishmael are characters in which novel?

- O *Moby-Dick*
- O *The Great Gatsby*
- O *East of Eden*

116. What is the popular name of Beethoven's Third Symphony?

- O Pastoral
- O Emperor
- O Eroica

117. In December 1920, which author published an article in the *Strand* magazine in which he expressed his belief in the existence of fairies?

- O Arthur Conan Doyle
- O Edgar Rice Burroughs
- O H. Rider Haggard

118. Which writer accidentally shot and killed his wife in Mexico in 1951?

- O Jack Kerouac
- O William Burroughs
- O Charles Bukowski

119. Which writer and director created the 1977 play *Abigail's Party*?

- O Ken Loach
- O Mike Leigh
- O Alan Clarke

120. *The Screaming Popes* is a series of works by which twentieth-century artist?

- O David Hockney
- O Lucian Freud
- O Francis Bacon

121. The maxim, 'He who can, does; he who cannot, teaches,' is taken from a comedy by which playwright?

O Noël Coward

O George Bernard Shaw

O J. B. Priestley

122. The artist Tracey Emin was brought up in which seaside resort?

O Skegness

O Blackpool

O Margate

123. Mick, Aston and the tramp Davies are characters in which Harold Pinter play?

O *The Caretaker*

O *The Birthday Party*

O *The Homecoming*

124. *The Sorcerer's Apprentice* is a work by which French composer?

O Chopin

O Berlioz

O Dukas

125. *The Bridal Chorus*, commonly known as 'Here Comes The Bride', is a piece of music by which composer?

O Wagner

O Brahms

O Mussorgsky

126. Which American author is particularly known for wearing a pristine white suit?

O John Irving

O John Updike

O Tom Wolfe

127. *The Buddha of Suburbia* is a book by which writer?

- O Hanif Kureishi
- O Zadie Smith
- O Salman Rushdie

128. Where was the sculptor Henry Moore born?

- O Castleford
- O Neath
- O Aberdeen

129. What was founded in 1946 by Sir Thomas Beecham?

- O The Royal Philharmonic Orchestra
- O The Ballet Rambert
- O The Aldeburgh Festival

130. The Rijksmuseum is a celebrated art gallery located in which country?

- O Germany
- O Belgium
- O Netherlands

131. What is the pen name of the writer David Cornwell?

- O Len Deighton
- O Jack Higgins
- O John Le Carré

132. *'Tis* and *Teacher Man* are books by which writer?

- O Frank McCourt
- O J. P. Donleavy
- O Roddy Doyle

133. Which artist, born in 1887, once controversially exhibited a urinal entitled *Fountain*?

- O Salvador Dalí
- O Marcel Duchamp
- O Pablo Picasso

134. Seamus Heaney won the 1999 Whitbread Prize for his translation of a poem about which mythical character?

- O Beowulf
- O Odysseus
- O Gilgamesh

135. What name is traditionally given to the period of artistic history between 1600 and 1750?

- O Classical
- O Baroque
- O Romantic

136. *Dealer's Choice* and *Closer* are plays by which contemporary writer?

- O Mark Ravenhill
- O Irvine Welsh
- O Patrick Marber

137. Which literary character was based upon Dr Joseph Bell, a professor at the University of Edinburgh Medical School?

- O Hercule Poirot
- O Sherlock Holmes
- O Jules Maigret

138. 'I Sing the Body Electric' is a poem by which American author?

- O Walt Whitman
- O Robert Lowell
- O John Berryman

139. Which Van Gogh painting was sold for a record $82.5 million in 1990?

- O *The Portrait of Dr Gachet*
- O *Wheatfield with Crows*
- O *Red Vineyard*

140. What is the title of the W. H. Davies poem that contains the lines, 'What is this life if full of care we have no time to stand and stare'?

- O Play
- O Sloth
- O Leisure

141. Which book by Iain Banks features the disturbed siblings Eric and Frank Cauldhame?

- O *The Wasp Factory*
- O *The Crow Road*
- O *Dead Air*

142. 'My heart aches, and a drowsy numbness pains, My sense, as though of hemlock I had drunk,' are the opening lines of which work by John Keats?

- O Ode to a Nightingale
- O The Eve of St Agnes
- O Hyperion

143. What does the P stand for in the name of the *Mary Poppins* author P. L. Travers?

- O Priscilla
- O Prudence
- O Pamela

144. What is the title of the 1968 James Bond novel written by Kingsley Amis?

- O *Colonel Sun*
- O *Icebreaker*
- O *Death Is For Ever*

145. The Benjamin Britten opera *Peter Grimes* is based on a poem by which East Anglian writer?

- O Edward Fitzgerald
- O Mark Akenside
- O George Crabbe

146. What is the full name of the title character in the Eugene O'Neill play *The Iceman Cometh*?

- O Theodore Hickman
- O Ezra Mannon
- O James Tyrone

147. Which French writer famously declined the 1964 Nobel Prize for Literature?

- O Albert Camus
- O Jean-Paul Sartre
- O Jean Genet

148. Who wrote the 1912 book entitled *Death in Venice*?

- O Thomas Mann
- O Noël Coward
- O D. H. Lawrence

149. What is the name of the Finch family cook in Harper Lee's novel *To Kill a Mockingbird*?

- O Calpurnia
- O Cecilia
- O Cressida

150. *The Man Who Mistook His Wife for a Hat* is an opera by which composer?

- O Harrison Birtwistle
- O Philip Glass
- O Michael Nyman

Answers on p.283

General Knowledge

1. By what name is the rapper Marshall Mathers III better known?

- O Eminem
- O Ludacris
- O 50 Cent

2. What type of animal is an Aberdeen Angus?

- O Pig
- O Cow
- O Horse

3. What are traditionally made by milliners?

- O Hats
- O Furniture
- O Farm Machinery

4. The Golden Palm, or the Palm d'Or, is a prestigious award at which film festival?

- O Cannes
- O Venice
- O Berlin

5. Mount Fuji is the highest mountain in which country?

- O Japan
- O China
- O Thailand

6. With which instrument would you associate the musician James Galway?

- O Guitar
- O Violin
- O Flute

7. Which organization was the subject of Simon Goodenough's 1977 book *All Jam and Jerusalem*?

- O The Salvation Army
- O The Scouts
- O The Women's Institute

8. The pop singer Bjork was born in which country?

- O Germany
- O Denmark
- O Iceland

9. Who said, 'Free at last, free at last. Thank God almighty, we are free at last,' in August 1963?

- O Martin Luther King
- O Malcolm X
- O John F. Kennedy

10. Which biblical patriarch died at the ripe old age of 969?

- O Abraham
- O Noah
- O Methuselah

11. The multi-millionaire William Randolph Hearst is reputed to be the inspiration for the 1941 film?

- O *Citizen Kane*
- O *John D. Rockefeller*
- O *J. P. Morgan*

12. The Eightfold Path leading to Nirvana is a belief central to which religion?

- O Buddhism
- O Sikhism
- O Islam

13. What was the name of the wheelchair-bound character played by Peter Kay in the TV sitcom *Phoenix Nights*?

- O Jerry St Clair
- O Ray Von
- O Brian Potter

14. Idi Amin seized control of which African country in 1971?

- O Uganda
- O Chad
- O Nigeria

15. Which businessman wiped an estimated £500 million off the value of his company by admitting in a 1991 speech that the products he sold were 'crap'?

- O Gerald Ratner
- O Alan Sugar
- O James Goldsmith

16. Who won the 2007 series of *Celebrity Big Brother*?

- O Bez
- O Shilpa Shetty
- O Mark Owen

17. Who was the lead singer of the Commodores?

- O Marvin Gaye
- O Sam Cooke
- O Lionel Ritchie

18. Phil 'The Power' Taylor is a leading figure in which sport?

- O Snooker
- O Darts
- O Boxing

19. The fashion designer Manolo Blahnik is best known for manufacturing which items of clothing?

- O Coats
- O Suits
- O Shoes

20. In which year did Diego Maradona score his infamous 'Hand of God' goal against England?

- O 1982
- O 1986
- O 1990

21. What is the alternative name for a Gnu?

- O Wildebeest
- O Ostrich
- O Giraffe

22. What does the W stand for in the name of George W. Bush?

- O Wade
- O Winston
- O Walker

23. True cockneys are supposed to be born within earshot of the bells of which Cheapside church?

- O St Mary-le-Bow
- O St Martin-in-the-Fields
- O St Paul's Cathedral

24. In France, what disease is referred to as *la rage*?

- O Tuberculosis
- O Leprosy
- O Rabies

25. What was the catchphrase of the TV policeman Kojak?

- 'Who loves ya, baby?'
- 'Book 'em, Danno.'
- 'Let's be careful out there.'

26. Adrian Moorhouse won an Olympic gold medal in which sport?

- Rowing
- Swimming
- Sailing

27. 'I love the smell of napalm in the morning,' is a quote from which 1979 film?

- *Apocalypse Now*
- *The Deer Hunter*
- *Coming Home*

28. Which manager of the England football team was ridiculed in the media for his close association with the faith healer Eileen Drewery?

- Kevin Keegan
- Glenn Hoddle
- Terry Venables

29. Which criminal of the Old West was shot dead by Pat Garrett in 1881?

- John Wesley Hardin
- Butch Cassidy
- Billy the Kid

30. Which African port is at the northern end of the Suez Canal?

- Port Said
- Alexandria
- Benghazi

31. The Silver Ghost and Silver Dawn were cars manufactured by which company?

- O Aston Martin
- O Bentley
- O Rolls Royce

32. Which singer courted controversy by invading the stage at the 1996 Brit Awards during a performance by Michael Jackson?

- O Liam Gallagher
- O Brandon Block
- O Jarvis Cocker

33. In which year did the Pilgrim Fathers set sail for America in the *Mayflower*?

- O 1520
- O 1620
- O 1720

34. The name of which animal is used to describe the dynamic economies of countries such as Singapore or Taiwan?

- O Tiger
- O Lion
- O Panther

35. In which month is Burns' Night annually celebrated?

- O January
- O March
- O June

36. Jan Ludvik Hoch was the original name of which controversial businessman?

- O Rupert Murdoch
- O Kerry Packer
- O Robert Maxwell

37. Chorlton-Cum-Hardy is a suburb of which English city?

- O Manchester
- O Liverpool
- O Bradford

38. The selection of which cricketer in England's 1968 touring party led to South Africa's exclusion from test match cricket?

- O Basil D'Oliveira
- O Norman Cowans
- O Wilf Slack

39. 'The Big Easy' is the official nickname of which US city?

- O St Louis
- O Atlanta
- O New Orleans

40. Which weatherman fatefully said in October 1987, 'A woman rang to say she heard there was a hurricane on the way. Well don't worry, there isn't'?

- O John Kettley
- O Michael Fish
- O Ian McCaskill

41. What is the technical term for the human breastbone?

- O Sternum
- O Clavicle
- O Scapula

42. The Aswan High Dam controls the flooding of which river?

- O Niger
- O Amazon
- O Nile

43. What did a fletcher traditionally make?

- O Barrels
- O Arrows
- O Wagons

44. Which football manager said, 'Some people think that football is a matter of life or death; I am very disappointed with that attitude. I can assure you it is much more important than that'?

- O Bill Shankly
- O Brian Clough
- O Alf Ramsey

45. The notorious gangster Bugsy Siegel is regarded as one of the founding fathers of which US city?

- O Las Vegas
- O Los Angeles
- O San Francisco

46. Which pre-decimal coin was known colloquially as the 'tanner'?

- O Sixpence
- O Pound
- O Penny

47. In Irish folklore, the wailing of which mythological creatures prophesy the death of a family member?

- O Banshee
- O Leprechaun
- O Fomorian

48. What role does a gaffer perform on a film set?

- O Wardobe assistant
- O Photographer
- O Electrician

49. What name is given to the river Thames within the city of Oxford?

- O Isis
- O Juno
- O Lug

50. What number is assigned to Patrick McGoohan in the cult TV series *The Prisoner*?

- O Twenty-one
- O Fifteen
- O Six

51. Which boxer became heavyweight champion of the world in 2001 by defeating Lennox Lewis in South Africa?

- O Hasim Rahman
- O James 'Buster' Douglas
- O Riddick Bowe

52. In Greek legend, who was the ferryman who carried the souls of the dead across the river Styx?

- O Charon
- O Tartarus
- O Lethe

53. In 2001, the Great Train Robber Ronnie Biggs returned from exile in which country?

- O Australia
- O Thailand
- O Brazil

54. Who became the president of the United States National Rifle Association in 1998?

- O Charlton Heston
- O Clint Eastwood
- O Kirk Douglas

55. Maastricht is a town in which European country?

- Italy
- Germany
- Netherlands

56. Which former Soviet nation is sometimes referred to as 'White Russia'?

- Belarus
- Chechnya
- Azerbaijan

57. Which comic book superhero was created by Joe Shuster and Jerry Siegel?

- Spider-Man
- Batman
- Superman

58. 'Lady Day' was the nickname of which jazz and blues singer?

- Billie Holiday
- Ella Fitzgerald
- Sarah Vaughan

59. Which comedian was cleared of charges of tax evasion in 1989?

- Ken Dodd
- Jimmy Tarbuck
- Frank Carson

60. According to popular legend, the monarchy will fall if which birds leave the Tower of London?

- Blackbirds
- Ravens
- Magpies

61. Which small European state has a total area of less than one square mile?

- Luxembourg
- Monaco
- Andorra

62. Which form of therapy takes its name from the Japanese for 'finger pressure'?

- Shiatsu
- Reiki
- Yoga

63. Which river forms much of the boundary between the United States and Mexico?

- Rio Grande
- Missouri
- Hudson

64. What was the name of the college band that featured a young Tony Blair on guitar?

- Loose Talk
- Hot Gossip
- Ugly Rumours

65. Bill Clinton was governor of which US state before becoming president?

- Arkansas
- Georgia
- Florida

66. Which motorway runs between Liverpool and Manchester?

- M62
- M18
- M4

67. Which musical is based on T. H. White's book *The Once and Future King*?

- O *Man of La Mancha*
- O *Camelot*
- O *Miss Saigon*

68. The West Yorkshire town of Pontefract is famous for producing what type of confectionery?

- O Chocolate
- O Marshmallow
- O Liquorice

69. Which performer, when asked whether critical disdain to his work upset him, replied, 'Oh yes . . . I cry all the way to the bank'?

- O Liberace
- O Benny Hill
- O David Hasselhoff

70. Guru Nanak was the founder of which religion?

- O Islam
- O Sikhism
- O Buddhism

71. Which star of the silver screen said, 'It's not the men in my life that count – it's the life in my men'?

- O Marlene Dietrich
- O Mae West
- O Tallulah Bankhead

72. What was the first name of Lawrence of Arabia?

- O Edmund
- O Thomas
- O Henry

73. Members of the British Army regiment known as the Gurkhas are recruited from the hill tribes of which country?

- O Pakistan
- O Nepal
- O Cambodia

74. In which country did the first human heart transplant take place in 1967?

- O Swaziland
- O South Africa
- O Lesotho

75. What colour are the leaves of the turmeric plant?

- O Blue
- O Yellow
- O Pink

76. Which children's TV series always ended with one character uttering the line, 'Time for bed'?

- O *Bagpuss*
- O *Mr Ben*
- O *The Magic Roundabout*

77. Prince Edward resigned from which military regiment in the 1980s?

- O Marines
- O SAS
- O Black Watch

78. What is the meaning of the word 'poltergeist', when translated from the German?

- O Home invader
- O Noisy spirit
- O Evil presence

79. *Helianthus* is the Latin name for which flower?

- O Venus Fly Trap
- O Daffodil
- O Sunflower

80. What is the name of the associated women's college at Harvard University?

- O Radcliffe College
- O Bryn Mawr
- O Columbia College

81. What name, inspired by the US president of the time, was given to the shanty towns that sprang up in the US during the Great Depression?

- O Wilsonvilles
- O Hoovervilles
- O Trumanvilles

82. In July 1982, Michael Fagan broke into the bedroom of which public figure?

- O The Queen
- O The US President
- O The Dalai Lama

83. 'I could have had class. I could have been a contender,' is a famous line first spoken by Marlon Brando in which 1954 film?

- O *A Streetcar Named Desire*
- O *The Men*
- O *On the Waterfront*

84. The Anglo-Saxon burial ground of Sutton Hoo is located in which English county?

- O Cumbria
- O Suffolk
- O Cornwall

85. 'That's Entertainment' was a UK hit single in 1981 for which band?

- O Madness
- O The Specials
- O The Jam

86. *The Prince* is a 1513 book by which writer and statesman?

- O Niccolò Machiavelli
- O Cesare Borgia
- O Casanova

87. Which former England cricket captain was made the Bishop of Liverpool in 1975?

- O Gubby Allen
- O Pelham Warner
- O David Sheppard

88. What type of mining is traditionally carried out in a 'stannary' area?

- O Tin
- O Coal
- O Diamond

89. 'The Thunderer' is an old-fashioned nickname for which newspaper?

- O *Guardian*
- O *The Times*
- O *Daily Mail*

90. Which British horse racing town is also the name of a card game?

- O Great Yarmouth
- O Newmarket
- O Redcar

91. In 1941, James Stewart won the only Best Actor Oscar of his career for which film?

- *Harvey*
- *The Philadelphia Story*
- *Bend of the River*

92. In religious legend, who performed the dance of the seven veils and demanded the head of John the Baptist?

- Delilah
- Jezebel
- Salome

93. The French title *chevalier* was originally an equivalent to which rank of British nobility?

- Earl
- Knight
- Baron

94. Lime Street is the name of the railway station of which English city?

- Liverpool
- Sheffield
- Norwich

95. Noël Coward implored which woman not to put her daughter 'on the stage' in a celebrated 1935 song?

- Mrs Wellington
- Mrs Warburton
- Mrs Worthington

96. Which comic actor represented Cambridge University in the 1980 Boat Race?

- Tony Slattery
- Rory McGrath
- Hugh Laurie

97. In 1927, who made the first ever solo non-stop transatlantic flight?

- O Amelia Earhart
- O Charles Lindbergh
- O Howard Hughes

98. Romansch is one of the official languages of which European country?

- O Austria
- O Luxembourg
- O Switzerland

99. In 1883, the original *Orient Express* began its first passenger journey from which city?

- O London
- O Madrid
- O Paris

100. The colourful pearly kings and queens of London traditionally did which job for a living?

- O Costermonger
- O Butcher
- O Confectioner

101. In Greek mythology, who solved the riddle of the Sphinx?

- O Odysseus
- O Orpheus
- O Oedipus

102. Who wrote a 1946 book entitled *The Common Sense Book of Baby and Child Care*?

- O John Nash
- O Benjamin Spock
- O Alfred Kinsey

103. Which item of clothing is referred to by the Russian word *babushka*, meaning 'grandmother'?

- O Headscarf
- O Overcoat
- O Cardigan

104. Which male tennis player won three of the four major tennis singles' titles in 1974?

- O John McEnroe
- O Jimmy Connors
- O Ilie Nastase

105. Which cartoonist created the unruly schoolgirls of St Trinian's?

- O Gerald Scarfe
- O Ralph Steadman
- O Ronald Searle

106. Which British prime minister conducted a brutal cabinet reshuffle known as 'The Night of the Long Knives' in the 1960s?

- O Harold Macmillan
- O Anthony Eden
- O Harold Wilson

107. Tric-trac is an alternative version of which board game?

- Backgammon
- Ludo
- Chess

108. What is the highest rank in the British army?

- O General
- O Commodore
- O Field Marshal

109. Castel Gandolfo is an official residence of which public figure?

- *O* Pope
- *O* Dalai Lama
- *O* Italian Prime Minister

110. Speaker's Corner is a feature of which of London's Parks?

- *O* Hyde Park
- *O* Regent's Park
- *O* Green Park

111. The comic actress Hattie Jacques married which star of *Dad's Army* in 1949?

- *O* Clive Dunn
- *O* Ian Lavender
- *O* John Le Mesurier

112. What is the name of Ian Fleming's Jamaican mansion where he wrote many of his James Bond novels?

- *O* Moonraker
- *O* Octopussy
- *O* Goldeneye

113. Eton College was founded in 1440 by which English king?

- *O* Richard III
- *O* Edward VI
- *O* Henry VI

114. In the seventeenth century, which philosopher famously declared, 'I think, therefore I am'?

- *O* René Descartes
- *O* John Locke
- *O* Thomas Paine

115. Van Diemen's Land is the former name of which island?

- O Madagascar
- O Tasmania
- O Mauritius

116. Which member of the British Royal Family was victim to an abduction attempt whilst being driven down the Mall in 1974?

- O Princess Anne
- O The Queen
- O Prince Charles

117. In popular legend, who was supposed to have cut the Gordian Knot?

- O Hannibal
- O Julius Caesar
- O Alexander the Great

118. Which of the world's seas is considered to be the largest lake in the world?

- O Black Sea
- O Caspian Sea
- O Baltic Sea

119. In 1942, Mickey Rooney married which actress?

- O Ava Gardner
- O Katharine Hepburn
- O Greta Garbo

120. The body of which British mountaineer was found on Mount Everest in May 1999?

- O George Leigh Mallory
- O Peter Boardman
- O Jack Longland

121. Which former Wimbledon champion did Billie Jean King defeat in the much-hyped 'Battle of the Sexes' in Houston in 1973?

- O Bobby Riggs
- O Bill Tilden
- O Don Budge

122. The American Jennie Jerome was the mother of which British prime minister?

- O Chamberlain
- O Churchill
- O Bonar Law

123. Which former world heavyweight boxing champion was known as the 'Easton Assassin'?

- O Larry Holmes
- O Floyd Patterson
- O Leon Spinks

124. The M69 motorway runs between Coventry and which city?

- O Leicester
- O Norwich
- O Swindon

125. Which actor won the first ever Best Actor Oscar in 1929?

- O John Barrymore
- O Lon Chaney
- O Emil Jannings

126. 'The law is an ass!' is a line from which Charles Dickens novel?

- O *Oliver Twist*
- O *David Copperfield*
- O *Nicholas Nickleby*

127. The Hansard Reports chronicle events that occur in which field?

- O Sport
- O Art
- O Politics

128. The Bodleian Library is part of which university?

- O Oxford
- O Harvard
- O The Sorbonne

129. 'Fiend angelical' and 'deafening silence' are examples of which contradictory figure of speech?

- O Oxymoron
- O Onomatopoeia
- O Assonance

130. What symbol is traditionally used to signify the election of a new pope?

- O White smoke
- O Red flag
- O Green fireworks

131. Which Hindu deity is known as 'The Destroyer'?

- O Shiva
- O Brahma
- O Vishnu

132. What was the name of the vessel in which Francis Chichester travelled solo around the world in 1967 and 1968?

- O *Kingfisher*
- O *Gypsy Moth IV*
- O *Challenger II*

133. Which singer was arrested in the 1970s for withholding her taxes in protest at the Vietnam War?

- O Aretha Franklin
- O Dionne Warwick
- O Nina Simone

134. The Christmas tree that stands in Trafalgar Square during the holiday season is traditionally a gift from which country?

- O Norway
- O Denmark
- O Germany

135. The 'New Look' of 1947 is an influential collection by which fashion designer?

- O Givenchy
- O Chanel
- O Dior

136. In 1963, the volcanic islet of Surtsey appeared off the coast of which country?

- O Denmark
- O Sweden
- O Iceland

137. Which British pastime is known in the US as 'spelunking'?

- O Bird watching
- O Potholing
- O Hang gliding

138. In terms of area, what is the smallest US state?

- O Rhode Island
- O Hawaii
- O Alaska

139. From which animal is eiderdown traditionally obtained?

- O Duck
- O Swan
- O Goose

140. What was invented by Percy Shaw in 1934?

- O Microwave oven
- O Cat's eyes
- O Digital calculator

141. Which inventor first said, 'Genius is one per cent inspiration and ninety-nine per cent perspiration'?

- O Wallace Carrothers
- O Isaac Newton
- O Thomas Edison

142. Who won a Best Director Oscar in both 1976 and 1985?

- O Francis Ford Coppola
- O Peter Bogdanovich
- O Milos Forman

143. Which author scripted the first ever royal Christmas speech, delivered by George V in 1932?

- O Thomas Hardy
- O Rudyard Kipling
- O Graham Greene

144. The seventeenth-century poet Sir John Suckling invented which card game?

- O Bridge
- O Poker
- O Cribbage

145. Traveller's Joy and Old Man's Beard are varieties of which plant?

- O Clematis
- O Snapdragon
- O Begonia

146. Which British Army unit was founded by David Sterling during the Second World War?

- O Black Watch
- O Marines
- O SAS

147. The Frenchman Gilles de Rais is traditionally associated with which figure from European folklore?

- O Bluebeard
- O The Pied Piper
- O William Tell

148. The former tennis player Pam Shriver married which actor in 2002?

- O Robert Vaughan
- O George Lazenby
- O James Coburn

149. Which journalist was labelled 'The First Man in Stanley' by the *Evening Standard* after sneaking in to Argentinean-held Port Stanley during the Falklands conflict?

- O John Simpson
- O Michael Peschardt
- O Max Hastings

150. Which intellectual and counter-culture icon coined the phrase, 'Turn on, tune in and drop out,' in a 1966 lecture?

- O Timothy Leary
- O Allen Ginsberg
- O Ken Kesey

DAPHNE FOWLER Food & Drink

Full name:
Daphne Fowler

Home town:
Born in Warwick, Daphne now lives in Somerset.

Education:
Studied Theology at Exeter University.

Quizzing credentials:
1979 Contestant on *Winner Takes All*
1983 Winner of a Mini car on *Sale of the Century*
1997 Crowned Radio 4's *Brain of Britain*
2000 *One to Win*
2000–02 *15–1*

Strongest Eggheads subject:
Food and Drink

Least favourite subject:
Despite it being her strongest subject, Daphne isn't keen on Food and Drink as a category. She also is tone deaf so dislikes anything that requires recognizing tunes.

Special interest:
Detective novels and biographies. Her favourite author is P. D. James.

Answers on p.285

Food & Drink

1. Tapas is a style of food originating in which country?

- *O* Greece
- *O* Romania
- *O* Spain

2. Which type of spirit is traditionally drunk in 'shots' accompanied by salt and sliced lemons?

- *O* Tequila
- *O* Vodka
- *O* Absinthe

3. Scampi is traditionally made with which type of seafood?

- *O* Salmon
- *O* Prawn
- *O* Scallop

4. What foodstuff provides the basis for the dish Guacamole?

- *O* Fish roe
- *O* Cucumber
- *O* Avocado

5. Which sandwich filling was favoured by Paddington Bear?

- *O* Marmalade
- *O* Honey
- *O* Tomato ketchup

6. Which chicken dish is named after a battle won by Napoleon that took place on 14 June 1800?

- *O* Marengo
- *O* Copenhagen
- *O* Valmy

7. What is the literal meaning of the popular dessert crème brulée?

- *O* Whipped cream
- *O* Burnt cream
- *O* Chilled cream

8. Which word in Italian cookery, literally meaning 'before the meal', is used to describe cold hors d'oeuvres?

- *O* Aioli
- *O* Secondi
- *O* Antipasti

9. In 1997, the TV cook Delia Smith became a director of which football club?

- *O* Ipswich Town
- *O* Norwich City
- *O* Cambridge United

10. In Scottish cookery, a haggis is traditionally made with the heart, liver and lungs of which animal?

- *O* Pig
- *O* Sheep
- *O* Horse

11. Which vegetable is a national symbol of Wales?

- *O* Turnip
- *O* Carrot
- *O* Leek

12. In 1988, who was the junior health minister who claimed that most of Britain's eggs were infected with salmonella?

- *O* Teresa Gorman
- *O* Edwina Currie
- *O* Ann Widdecombe

13. 'Thermidor' and 'Newburg' are traditional methods of cooking which marine creature?

- O Lobster
- O Salmon
- O Mussels

14. Stollen is a type of Christmas cake made with dried fruit from which country?

- O Germany
- O Portugal
- O Egypt

15. Colcannon is a type of mashed potato traditionally made in which country?

- O France
- O Sweden
- O Ireland

16. Mozzarella cheese was originally made from the milk of which animal?

- O Sheep
- O Goat
- O Buffalo

17. By what name is crème anglaise better known?

- O Grain mustard
- O Custard
- O Cranberry jelly

18. The dish called 'succotash' was originally made by which people?

- O Native Americans
- O Inuits
- O Australian Aborigines

19. Which spirit is added to tomato juice to make a Bloody Mary cocktail?

- O Vodka
- O Rum
- O Gin

20. A nectarine is a smooth-skinned variant of which fruit?

- O Kiwi fruit
- O Pomegranate
- O Peach

21. Malaysian satay is traditionally served with what type of sauce?

- O Black bean
- O Oyster
- O Peanut

22. Which vegetables are traditionally served with cream and cheese 'à la dauphinoise'?

- O Cucumbers
- O Potatoes
- O Aubergines

23. The rice variety called 'basmati' was originally grown in the foothills of which range of mountains?

- O Himalayas
- O Alps
- O Rockies

24. Which term refers to the act of immersing food quickly in boiling water?

- O Blanching
- O Barding
- O Basting

25. Napoleon and Morello are varieties of which fruit?

- O Cherry
- O Pear
- O Apple

26. What type of nut is traditionally used to flavour a 'macaroon' biscuit?

- O Almond
- O Hazelnut
- O Cashew

27. What is Ouzo?

- O French pastry
- O German sausage
- O A Greek spirit

28. Jarlsberg cheese is a speciality of which country?

- O Norway
- O Romania
- O Spain

29. What kind of dessert is named after a ballet dancer born in 1881?

- O Pavlova
- O Nijinsky
- O Fonteyn

30. What is the main ingredient of the French dish 'bouillabaisse'?

- O Lamb
- O Veal
- O Fish

31. What type of dish is the Indian 'mulligatawny'?

- O Soup
- O Fish pie
- O Spicy vegetable kebab

32. Gin is traditionally flavoured with the berry-like cones of which tree?

- O Mulberry
- O Elderberry
- O Juniper

33. Popular in Cajun cookery, Muscadines and Scuppernongs are varieties of which foodstuff?

- O Grapes
- O Apples
- O Lemons

34. What type of food is 'brown Windsor'?

- O Soup
- O Chocolate cake
- O A beef pasty

35. In Italian cookery, what type of food is 'focaccia'?

- O Salad
- O Bread
- O Veal escalope

36. Eve's Pudding is a dessert traditionally made with which fruit?

- O Apple
- O Orange
- O Plum

Answers on p.285

37. What name is given to game dishes that are named in honour of the Roman goddess of the hunt?

- O Juno
- O Diane
- O Minerva

38. Which spice is the predominant flavouring of Hungarian goulash?

- O Saffron
- O Paprika
- O Mace

39. Which dish, inspired by the cuisine of China, was first made popular in August 1896, in New York City?

- O Chow Mein
- O Chop Suey
- O Peking Duck

40. Which type of coffee is named after the cowls worn by an order of monks established in 1525?

- O Latte
- O Cappuccino
- O Espresso

41. The Bakewell tart is named after a town in which English county?

- O Derbyshire
- O Kent
- O Devon

42. Which typically English food is often referred to as an 'oggy'?

- O Eccles cake
- O Yorkshire pudding
- O Cornish pasty

43. A Mint Julep cocktail is traditionally made with which type of spirit?

- O Vodka
- O Rum
- O Bourbon

44. When describing champagne, what does the term Brut stand for?

- O Sweet
- O Fizzy
- O Very dry

45. Bergamot essence is a traditional ingredient of which popular tea?

- O Earl Grey
- O Lapsang Souchong
- O Oolong

46. Which British film maker, born in 1935, is a restaurant critic in the *Sunday Times*?

- O Ken Russell
- O Michael Winner
- O Richard Attenborough

47. What is the name of the monk who is often credited with inventing champagne?

- O Bollinger
- O Taittinger
- O Perignon

48. The Mexican speciality of 'burritos' are named after which animal?

- O Donkey
- O Seagull
- O Monkey

49. What is the name of the green paste, similar to horseradish, used in Japanese cookery?

- *O* Sashimi
- *O* Ramen
- *O* Wasabi

50. Which herb traditionally forms the basis of a 'pesto' sauce?

- *O* Basil
- *O* Fennel
- *O* Coriander

51. In the Turkish dish 'dolmas', rice and lamb are wrapped in what?

- *O* Filo pastry
- *O* Ham
- *O* Vine leaves

52. What is the main ingredient of the Scottish dish 'stovied tatties'?

- *O* Haggis
- *O* Potato
- *O* Turnip

53. What is the name of the clarified butter widely used in Indian cuisine?

- *O* Ghee
- *O* Paneer
- *O* Roti

54. In which country is Bardolino wine produced?

- *O* Italy
- *O* Spain
- *O* Greece

55. In Italian cuisine, what is the name of the shell-shaped pasta?

- O Farfalle
- O Linguine
- O Conchiglie

56. People who subscribe to the controversial Atkins Diet minimize their intake of which of the major food groups?

- O Protein
- O Carbohydrate
- O Fat

57. The dish of 'bigos', traditionally made with sauerkraut and cooked meat, is a speciality of which country?

- O Ireland
- O Poland
- O Greece

58. The Italian city of Parma is particularly famous for the production of what?

- O Ice cream
- O Olive oil
- O Ham

59. In Italian cuisine, what are 'porcini'?

- O Mushrooms
- O Sun-dried tomatoes
- O Stuffed olives

60. What type of salad is traditionally made with tomato, olives and feta cheese?

- O Niçoise
- O Greek
- O Caesar

61. Ossetra and Sevruga are noted varieties of which delicacy?

- O Smoked salmon
- O Caviar
- O Truffle

62. Milk, vodka and which other alcoholic drink are used to make a White Russian cocktail?

- O Kahlua
- O Absinthe
- O Drambuie

63. What type of food is 'Cornish yarg'?

- O Cheese
- O Sausage meat
- O Fish pie

64. 'Wiener schnitzel' is a dish traditionally made in which country?

- O Italy
- O Switzerland
- O Austria

65. By what name is the 'fava bean' also known?

- O Broad bean
- O French bean
- O Runner bean

66. The American Deep South speciality known as 'chittlins' is made from which part of a pig?

- O Intestines
- O Tail
- O Feet

67. Colman's mustard was founded in the nineteenth century in which city?

O York

O Exeter

O Norwich

68. The Napa Valley is a wine-producing area in which American state?

O California

O Arizona

O Florida

69. Owing to the process involved in its manufacture, the name of which Italian cheese is translated as 'cooked again'?

O Ricotta

O Gorgonzola

O Mascarpone

70. Raki is the national drink of which country?

O Turkey

O Japan

O Egypt

71. 'Frittata' is an Italian version of which common dish?

O Omelette

O Steak and kidney pie

O Toad in the hole

72. What type of rum cocktail is named after a small village in the east of Cuba?

O Mai Tai

O Margarita

O Daiquiri

73. What are traditionally dried in an 'oast house'?

- O Meat
- O Oats
- O Hops

74. What type of nuts are traditionally used in a Waldorf salad?

- O Walnuts
- O Cashew nuts
- O Macadamia nuts

75. The traditional British breakfast dish called 'kedgeree' was originally devised in which country?

- O India
- O Australia
- O Cuba

76. Marsala wine was first produced on which Mediterranean island?

- O Crete
- O Sicily
- O Majorca

77. Which summer fruit provides the flavouring of the liqueur 'framboise'?

- O Raspberry
- O Blackberry
- O Redcurrant

78. What traditionally sticks out of the top of a 'stargazey pie'?

- O Fish heads
- O Rabbit feet
- O Deer antlers

79. In Italian cuisine, what is 'pecorino'?

- O Cheese
- O Pasta
- O Soup

80. What fruit is traditionally used to make the dish 'tarte tatin'?

- O Peach
- O Orange
- O Apple

81. What are poached in syrup and glazed in the delicacy of 'marrons glacés'?

- O Prunes
- O Chestnuts
- O Grapes

82. The liqueur 'cassis' is made from which fruit?

- O Blackcurrant
- O Apple
- O Pear

83. What is a French 'marmite'?

- O Cooking pot
- O Spice grinder
- O Baking tray

84. What drink is traditionally flavoured with the anti-malaria drug quinine?

- O Tonic water
- O Bitter lemon
- O Soda water

85. What is added to scotch to make the drink known as Whisky Mac?

- O Cola
- O Soda water
- O Ginger ale

86. What is the real name of the TV chef popularly known as 'The Galloping Gourmet'?

- O Robert Carrier
- O Graham Kerr
- O Fanny Cradock

87. Which vegetable provides the basis for any dish served 'du Barry'?

- O Carrot
- O Cauliflower
- O Aubergine

88. The Scandinavian dish of 'gravlax' is traditionally made with which fish?

- O Salmon
- O Herring
- O Monkfish

89. What is another name for the edible plant called the 'endive'?

- O Chive
- O Chicory
- O Artichoke

90. The Warwickshire Drooper and the Kirke's Blue are varieties of which fruit?

- O Plum
- O Peach
- O Pear

91. Which popular dessert takes its name from the German word for 'whirlpool'?

- O Linzer torte
- O Sachertorte
- O Strudel

92. The Barossa Valley is a wine-producing region in which country?

- O Italy
- O USA
- O Australia

93. Which Spanish dish is named after the cooking pot in which it is traditionally made?

- O Gazpacho
- O Paella
- O Mojama

94. Which of these cuts of beef is taken from an area just above the front legs of the animal?

- O Silverside
- O Brisket
- O Sirloin

95. In Northern Ireland, from what are 'fadge cakes' made?

- O Potato
- O Onion
- O Sponge

96. Madeira cake is traditionally made with the zest of which fruit?

- O Orange
- O Lime
- O Lemon

97. In the novel *Treasure Island*, the shipwrecked sailor Ben Gunn longed to eat which food?

- O Chocolate
- O Cheese
- O Roast beef

98. What spice is traditionally taken as a cure for seasickness?

- O Saffron
- O Ginger
- O Paprika

99. What type of food is Aspic?

- O Jelly
- O Pastry
- O Cooking Oil

100. The tea cakes called 'Sally Lunns' are named after a baker who lived in which English city?

- O Plymouth
- O Manchester
- O Bath

101. In Indian cuisine, what name is given to the salted or sweet yoghurt drink that is usually served with ice?

- O Murgh
- O Lassi
- O Karahi

102. What type of cocktail is traditionally made with bourbon, vermouth, a dash of bitters and garnished with a cherry?

- O Manhattan
- O Mimosa
- O Margarita

103. In Australia, with what is a 'carpetbag steak' stuffed?

- O Prunes
- O Prawns
- O Oysters

104. What type of drink is served by *baristas*?

- O Coffee
- O Champagne
- O Cocktails

105. Jambalaya is a speciality of which US city?

- O New Orleans
- O St Louis
- O Boston

106. What type of food is the Polish speciality 'borscht'?

- O Vegetable soup
- O Potato cake
- O Mushroom frittata

107. What name is given to traditional African-American dishes such as 'fried chicken' and 'collard greens'?

- O Funk food
- O Jazz food
- O Soul food

108. What food is wrapped in bacon in the dish of 'angels on horseback'?

- O Sausage
- O Oyster
- O Cheese

109. What word, also meaning bravery, is a collective term for the heart, liver and lungs of a slaughtered animal?

- O Valour
- O Mettle
- O Pluck

110. The Italian bread 'panettone' is traditionally eaten at which time of the year?

- O Christmas
- O Easter
- O Hallowe'en

111. What is the 'liquor' traditionally served with the East End of London speciality of pie and mash?

- O Tomato ketchup
- O Parsley sauce
- O Onion gravy

112. The word 'chutney' is derived from which language?

- O Arabic
- O Swahili
- O Hindi

113. A Harvey Wallbanger contains vodka, orange juice and which liqueur?

- O Galliano
- O Cointreau
- O Kahlua

114. The technique for opening a champagne bottle called 'sabrage' involves using which implement?

- O Sword
- O Hammer
- O Corkscrew

115. What name refers to hot toast spread with anchovy paste and topped with soft scrambled eggs?

- O English Woodcock
- O Welsh Woodcock
- O Scotch Woodcock

116. What type of food is 'lobscouse', from which Liverpudlians derive their popular nickname?

- O Steak
- O Sausage
- O Stew

117. In Indian cuisine, which curry is usually cooked with lentils and coriander?

- O Vindaloo
- O Dhansak
- O Korma

118. The lychee fruit is native to which country?

- O China
- O Russia
- O Mexico

119. What fruit is the traditional flavouring of 'crêpes suzette'?

- O Lemon
- O Tangerine
- O Melon

120. A Cheeky Vimto cocktail is made with vodka and a shot of which other ingredient?

- O Port
- O Brandy
- O Sherry

121. What type of cooking utensil is a skillet?

- *O* Sieve
- *O* Ladle
- *O* Frying pan

122. Which word refers to someone who is very fond of wine?

- *O* Oenophile
- *O* Arctophile
- *O* Pressophile

123. Which product was commercially introduced into Britain in 1930?

- *O* Processed cheese
- *O* Sliced bread
- *O* Baked beans

124. Which type of rice is traditionally used in making risotto?

- *O* Camargue
- *O* Pilau
- *O* Arborio

125. The common ingredient called cornflour is traditionally made from which cereal plant?

- *O* Maize
- *O* Barley
- *O* Wheat

126. The Horn of Plenty or Trumpet of Death is an example of which type of food?

- *O* Mushroom
- *O* Fruit
- *O* Cereal

127. The lime-based Caipirinha cocktail originated in which country?

- O Brazil
- O Cuba
- O Mexico

128. What was the name of the hen-pecked husband of the TV chef Fanny Cradock?

- O Jerry
- O Johnny
- O Jamie

129. The amber-coloured Tokay wine is traditionally made in which country?

- O South Africa
- O Hungary
- O Morocco

130. What is the name of the stomach lining of a cow, used to curdle milk in the production of cheese?

- O Tannin
- O Battin
- O Rennet

131. In Indian cuisine, what type of food is 'puri'?

- O Spinach
- O Unleavened bread
- O Cheese

132. In Jewish cuisine, what type of food is 'lox'?

- O Cured beef
- O Chicken
- O Salmon

133. The English delicacy known as 'Bath chap' is traditionally made from which part of a pig?

- Cheek
- Buttock
- Trotter

134. What is added to the French sandwich called the 'croque-monsieur' in order to make a 'croque-madame'?

- A baked egg
- Pickled onions
- Chutney

135. What type of beans is traditionally contained within a tin of baked beans?

- Kidney beans
- Haricot beans
- Butter beans

136. What is the Scoville Scale designed to measure?

- The fat content of a meal
- The strength of wine
- The heat of a chilli

137. What name is given to a bottle that contains approximately twelve litres of wine?

- Balthazar
- Jereboam
- Methuselah

138. Which popular English condiment is reputedly based on a recipe brought back from India by Marcus, Lord Sandys?

- Worcester sauce
- Tabasco
- Angostura bitters

139. Tiffin is a meal traditionally taken at which time of day?

- O Breakfast
- O Lunch
- O Supper

140. The word 'marmalade' comes from the Portuguese term for which fruit?

- O Quince
- O Tangelo
- O Lime

141. What type of food is the traditional Jewish delicacy 'matzo'?

- O Unleavened bread
- O Smoked salmon
- O Stuffed fish

142. What is the literal meaning of the name of the Swedish delicacy 'smorgasbord'?

- O Table of buttered bread
- O Halls of Valhalla
- O Field of herring

143. Which soup, particularly popular in Victorian cookery, is traditionally made with the head of a calf?

- O Cullen skink
- O Birds' nest soup
- O Mock turtle soup

144. What is the main ingredient in the dish called 'partan bree'?

- O Haggis
- O Crab meat
- O Venison

145. What type of food is the Maid of Honour, believed to have been invented by Anne Boleyn?

O Lemon and almond tart

O Cheese and chive flan

O Strawberry and blackberry mousse

146. The revered chef Auguste Escoffier joined the staff of which London hotel in 1890?

O The Ritz

O The Savoy

O Claridge's

147. The Dutch speciality known as 'rijsttafel' originated in which other country?

O Indonesia

O Thailand

O Madagascar

148. In Scottish cuisine, what is a 'bannock'?

O Smoked haddock

O Meat stew

O Oatcake

149. Which French cheese was reputedly invented during the French Revolution by a woman named Marie Harel?

O Port Salut

O Roquefort

O Camembert

150. What is the main ingredient of the Greek dish 'saganaki'?

O Cheese

O Lamb

O Aubergine

General Knowledge

1. Which Scottish village in Dumfries and Galloway is a famous destination for eloping English couples?

- *O* Dalkeith
- *O* Newtongrange
- *O* Gretna

2. By what name is the model Katie Price better known?

- *O* Jordan
- *O* Giselle
- *O* Caprice

3. The Queen's official birthday is in which month of the year?

- *O* January
- *O* June
- *O* October

4. The controversial Can-Can dance was first performed in which Parisian nightclub?

- *O* Moulin Rouge
- *O* The Lido
- *O* Le Caveau

5. In the USA, Thanksgiving is traditionally celebrated on the fourth Thursday of which month?

- *O* August
- *O* March
- *O* November

6. What is the English name for the day the French refer to as *Mardi Gras*?

- *O* Shrove Tuesday
- *O* Boxing Day
- *O* Midsummer's Day

7. By what name was the bodybuilder Angelo Siciliano better known?

- O Charles Atlas
- O The Incredible Hulk
- O Arnold Schwarzenegger

8. Who played the role of the evil wizard Saruman in Peter Jackson's *Lord of the Rings* trilogy?

- O Christopher Lee
- O Peter Cushing
- O Vincent Price

9. 'I Bet You Look Good On The Dancefloor' was a UK Number 1 hit single for which band?

- O Muse
- O Kaiser Chiefs
- O Arctic Monkeys

10. The M4 motorway runs between London and which city?

- O Leeds
- O Norwich
- O Swansea

11. Which year did the Queen famously refer to as her '*annus horribilus*' in her Christmas speech?

- O 1972
- O 1982
- O 1992

12. Traditionally, what household items would be made and sold by a chandler?

- O Candles
- O Chairs
- O Chimneys

13. Antonio Stradivari is best known for his skill in the manufacture of which musical instruments?

- Guitars
- Trumpets
- Violins

14. The fashion designer Jimmy Choo specializes in which item of clothing?

- Shoes
- Suits
- Hats

15. In which country was the late pope John Paul II born?

- Ireland
- Russia
- Poland

16. What precious gemstone is traditionally associated with a couple's fortieth wedding anniversary?

- Diamond
- Ruby
- Garnet

17. The statue of Helios known as the 'Colossus', one of the wonders of the ancient world, was located on which island?

- Rhodes
- Crete
- Malta

18. The English king Charles I was beheaded in which century?

- Thirteenth
- Seventeenth
- Nineteenth

19. *Justified* is the début solo album of which former boyband member?

- O Simon Webbe
- O Robbie Williams
- O Justin Timberlake

20. Petruchio and Katherine are bickering characters in which Shakespeare play?

- O *The Taming of the Shrew*
- O *Much Ado About Nothing*
- O *The Winter's Tale*

21. Which town in Arizona was the site of the Gunfight at the OK Corral?

- O Dodge City
- O Tombstone
- O Santa Fe

22. 'The Land Of My Fathers' is the national anthem of which country?

- O Scotland
- O Northern Ireland
- O Wales

23. Who did Jesus raise from the dead in the New Testament book of John?

- O Lazarus
- O John the Baptist
- O Herod Antipas

24. In mathematics, a kite has how many sides?

- O Two
- O Three
- O Four

25. 'Thank You' was a worldwide hit for which singer in 2004?

O Natasha Bedingfield

O Jamelia

O Kylie Minogue

26. The *War Cry* is the newsletter of which organization?

O Salvation Army

O Red Cross

O RSPCA

27. 'Oh, What A Beautiful Morning' is a song from which stage musical?

O *Carousel*

O *Oklahoma!*

O *Kismet*

28. John Logie Baird was a pioneer of which technological innovation?

O Television

O Telephone

O Microwave oven

29. Which county is traditionally known as 'The Garden of England'?

O Lincolnshire

O Cumbria

O Kent

30. In November 2000, who encased himself in a block of ice for more than two days?

O David Blaine

O Derren Brown

O David Copperfield

31. Which rapper features on Beyoncé Knowles' 2002 hit single 'Crazy In Love'?

- O P. Diddy
- O Jay-Z
- O Eminem

32. Cathay is a medieval name for which Asian country?

- O China
- O Russia
- O Thailand

33. The marine creature called the orca is better known by what name?

- O Great white shark
- O Killer whale
- O Octopus

34. In mathematics, what is the name given to a number that can only be divided by itself and one?

- O Imaginary number
- O Prime number
- O Square number

35. Haematology is the scientific name for the study of what?

- O Blood
- O Fungi
- O Skin

36. The poet Robert Burns was born in which country?

- O England
- O Wales
- O Scotland

37. The word 'ovine' specifically relates to which animals?

- O Sheep
- O Cows
- O Bears

38. What was the 'Penny Black'?

- O An overcoat
- O A car
- O A stamp

39. What did the actress Gwyneth Paltrow name her child, born on 14 May 2004?

- O Apple
- O Bluebell
- O Suri

40. On which day of the year is St Patrick's Day celebrated?

- O 17 March
- O 17 July
- O 17 October

41. Which girl's name with a French origin means 'beloved'?

- O Ellen
- O Amy
- O Doris

42. 'Give me your tired, your poor, your huddled masses yearning to breathe free,' are lines engraved on which famous landmark?

- O Sydney Opera House
- O Eiffel Tower
- O Statue of Liberty

43. Geronimo and Cochise were leaders of which Native American tribe?

- O Cherokee
- O Apache
- O Navaho

44. Joe Strummer was a singer and guitarist in which band?

- O The Sex Pistols
- O The Buzzcocks
- O The Clash

45. Which mountaineer, when asked in 1923 why he wanted to climb Everest replied, 'Because it's there'?

- O George Mallory
- O Edmund Hillary
- O John Hunt

46. Becher's Brook and The Chair are fences at which English racecourse?

- O Goodwood
- O Aintree
- O Newmarket

47. In Spanish dress, what is a 'bolero'?

- O Scarf
- O Dress
- O Jacket

48. In a game of Bingo, 'key of the door' is a traditional call for which number?

- O Sixteen
- O Twenty-one
- O Thirty-three

49. 'Frosty wind made moan,' is a line from which popular Christmas song written by Gustav Holst and Christina Rossetti?

- O The Twelve Days of Christmas
- O In The Bleak Midwinter
- O I Saw Three Ships Come Sailing By

50. The lavish San Simeon Estate in California was built by which eccentric millionaire?

- O William Randolph Hearst
- O Juan Trippe
- O John Paul Getty

51. 'Pine Tree' was the nickname of which former captain of the All Blacks Rugby Union team?

- O Colin Meads
- O Wayne Shelford
- O Zinzan Brooke

52. In which TV sitcom does Simon Pegg play the role of cartoonist Tim Bisley?

- O *Spaced*
- O *Peep Show*
- O *The IT Crowd*

53. 'All That Jazz' and 'Mr Cellophane' are songs featured in which stage musical?

- O *Chicago*
- O *Cabaret*
- O *Hello, Dolly*

54. Which explorer reputedly said, 'I am just going outside, and may be some time,' in 1912?

- O Captain Scott
- O Ernest Shackleton
- O Lawrence Oates

55. The Dow Jones Index traditionally indicates the prices of shares in the stock exchange of which city?

- O New York
- O Tokyo
- O Berlin

56. Who was the official photographer at the wedding of Prince Charles and Diana Spencer in 1981?

- O Terry O'Neill
- O David Bailey
- O Patrick Lichfield

57. The dance known as the Tango originated in which continent?

- O Asia
- O Europe
- O South America

58. Jemima Goldsmith married which cricketer in 1995?

- O Imran Khan
- O Wasim Akram
- O Javed Miandad

59. In terms of food additives, what does the E in E Numbers stand for?

- O European
- O Express
- O Engineered

60. The Trabant car, as featured on U2's *Achtung Baby* album cover, was traditionally made in which country?

- O East Germany
- O Spain
- O Hungary

61. The British Royal Mint is located in which country?

- O Scotland
- O Northern Ireland
- O Wales

62. In the Beatrix Potter book *The Tale of Peter Rabbit*, Peter sneaks into whose garden?

- O Mr McGregor
- O Mr McKenzie
- O Mr McGoohan

63. In 1972, Clifford Irving wrote a fake autobiography of which controversial businessman?

- O Howard Hughes
- O David O. Selznick
- O Sam Goldwyn

64. RTE is the state-owned national TV station of which country?

- O The Netherlands
- O France
- O Ireland

65. Who was the ancient Egyptian god of death?

- O Anubis
- O Hathor
- O Isis

66. 'We hold these truths to be self-evident, that all men are created equal,' is a fragment from which historical document?

- O The Communist Manifesto
- O The Magna Carta
- O The Declaration of Independence

67. The Pampa is a fertile plain in which of the world's continents?

- O South America
- O Africa
- O Asia

68. What magazine was set up in 1922 by DeWitt Wallace and his wife, Lila Acheson?

- O *Punch*
- O *Reader's Digest*
- O *Private Eye*

69. The tennis player Martina Navratilova was born in which European country?

- O Greece
- O Czechoslovakia
- O Romania

70. Which board game was invented by the out-of-work salesman Charles Darrow?

- O Monopoly
- O Scrabble
- O Risk

71. The *Mallard* and *Flying Scotsman* locomotives were built in which British town?

- O Doncaster
- O Barrow
- O Sunderland

72. In Greek mythology, what was the name of the world's first mortal woman?

- O Andromeda
- O Thisbe
- O Pandora

73. In the game of Contract Bridge, what is the lowest ranked of the four main card suits?

- O Spades
- O Clubs
- O Hearts

74. Wolfgang Amadeus Mozart was born in which city?

- O Rome
- O Budapest
- O Salzburg

75. 'Bamboos', 'circles', 'honours' and 'winds' are terms in which game?

- O Mah Jong
- O Cribbage
- O Backgammon

76. In Scotland, what is a Dashing White Sergeant?

- O A dance
- O A blood sausage
- O A mountain

77. Who are the rulers of a gerontocracy?

- O Animals
- O Old people
- O Doctors

78. Which politician was the owner of the Texas Rangers baseball team between 1989 and 1998?

- O Bill Clinton
- O Donald Rumsfeld
- O George W. Bush

79. Which monkey, also called the 'sapajou', is named after an order of monks?

- O Capuchin
- O Marmoset
- O Howler Monkey

80. What role did Sir Hardy Amies fulfil in the Queen's service?

- O Chef
- O Dressmaker
- O Stable master

81. The geyser known as 'Old Faithful' is a feature of which American national park?

- O Yosemite
- O Yellowstone
- O Mesa Verde

82. Jack Charlton played for which football club between 1952 and 1973?

- O Leeds United
- O Manchester United
- O Newcastle United

83. Which of these units of measurement is equal to three miles?

- O Fathom
- O Light year
- O League

84. What type of traditional Scottish highland weapon is a 'skean-dhu'?

- O Dagger
- O Broadsword
- O Mace

85. Prince Philip attended which British boarding school?

- O Harrow
- O Gordonstoun
- O Ampleforth

86. The independent Kingdom of Lesotho is completely surrounded by which other country?

- O Kenya
- O Nigeria
- O South Africa

87. In 1966, which member of the Beatles caused a furore by claiming, 'We're more popular than Jesus now'?

- O John Lennon
- O Paul McCartney
- O Ringo Starr

88. Who famously said, 'We have become a grandmother,' in 1989?

- O Margaret Thatcher
- O The Queen
- O Elizabeth Taylor

89. Jutland is an area in which European country?

- O Finland
- O Denmark
- O The Netherlands

90. The Scott Monument is a feature of which British city?

- O Cardiff
- O Belfast
- O Edinburgh

91. The politician David Mellor famously wore the shirt of which football team during his extra-marital tryst with Antonia de Sancha?

- O Chelsea
- O Fulham
- O Charlton Athletic

92. The original edition of the board game Monopoly was based on the streets of which US city?

- O Atlantic City
- O Boston
- O Philadelphia

93. What type of tree is featured on the flag of Lebanon?

- O Oak
- O Ash
- O Cedar

94. The Mazurka is a dance in triple time originating in which country?

- O Poland
- O Italy
- O Russia

95. Which comic book hero was created by Bob Kane?

- O Batman
- O The Punisher
- O Wolverine

96. Carl Bernstein and which other *Washington Post* journalist were instrumental in uncovering the 1974 Watergate scandal?

- O Bob Woodward
- O Jesse Helms
- O Tom Bowman

97. 'The Hippopotamus' is a song by which musical double act?

- O Chas and Dave
- O Renee and Renata
- O Flanders and Swann

98. To whom are people referring when they talk of 'the fourth estate'?

- O Journalists
- O The army
- O The aristocracy

99. Which Oscar-winning actor played the role of Roy Slater in the TV sitcom *Only Fools and Horses*?

- O Jim Broadbent
- O Michael Caine
- O Bill Nighy

100. Against which city did the Roman Empire wage the Punic Wars?

- O Syracuse
- O Athens
- O Carthage

101. 'The Andrew' is a nickname for which British military organization?

- O RAF
- O Army
- O Royal Navy

102. Which politician had a bucket of water thrown over him by a member of the pop group Chumbawumba at the 1998 Brit Awards?

- O Tony Blair
- O John Prescott
- O Jack Straw

103. Katana and Claymore are examples of which type of weapon?

- O Sword
- O Axe
- O Spear

104. Which musical instrument takes its name from the Hawaiian word for 'flea'?

- O Ukulele
- O Harmonica
- O Tambourine

105. In Greek legend, which king of Sparta was the husband of Helen of Troy?

- O Agamemnon
- O Menelaus
- O Odysseus

106. Which sportsman, born in 1934, is the first man to win world titles on motorbikes and in Formula 1?

- O Jackie Stewart
- O John Surtees
- O Jim Clark

107. The word 'pedagogy' relates specifically to the principles and practice of which profession?

- O Medicine
- O The Law
- O Teaching

108. Tynwald Court is the name of the parliament of which British island?

- O Jersey
- O Isle of Man
- O Anglesey

109. Who famously wrote in 1919 that, 'the female of the species is more deadly than the male'?

O Noël Coward

O Somerset Maugham

O Rudyard Kipling

110. What is the meaning of the word 'mensa' when translated from the Latin?

O Table

O Chair

O House

111. Who was the first woman to be awarded a perfect score of ten in Olympic gymnastic competition?

O Olga Korbut

O Nelli Kim

O Nadia Comaneci

112. Who plays the role of Bill in Quentin Tarantino's *Kill Bill* movies?

O Gene Hackman

O David Carradine

O Warren Beatty

113. The American Greg Louganis has won four Olympic gold medals in which event?

O Diving

O Skiing

O Athletics

114. What relation is the TV presenter, politician and gourmand Clement Freud to his psychoanalytical namesake Sigmund?

O Nephew

O Grandson

O Son

115. The Isle of Portland is a craggy peninsula on the coast of which English county?

- O Dorset
- O Cornwall
- O Devon

116. Which snooker player is nicknamed 'The Outlaw'?

- O Ronnie O'Sullivan
- O Joe Swail
- O John Higgins

117. In 1997, who succeeded Karl Lagerfeld as chief designer of the fashion house Chloë?

- O Stella McCartney
- O John Galliano
- O Alexander McQueen

118. Waverley and Haymarket are railway stations in which city?

- O Edinburgh
- O Newcastle-on-Tyne
- O Birmingham

119. The mode of transportation known as the 'bathysphere' was designed to travel in which environment?

- O Space
- O Underwater
- O Desert

120. What name is given to the Red Cross in Muslim countries?

- O Red Scimitar
- O Red Moon
- O Red Crescent

121. The Giant's Causeway in Northern Ireland is formed by columns of which rock?

- O Basalt
- O Quartz
- O Limestone

122. Which South African cricketer was banned from the sport for life in 2000 after admitting his involvement in match fixing?

- O Herschelle Gibbs
- O Hansie Cronje
- O Kepler Wessels

123. Who played the role of Clarence's father in the 1993 film *True Romance*?

- O Dennis Hopper
- O Peter Fonda
- O Jack Nicholson

124. Which cartoon strip was created by Bill Watterson?

- O *Calvin and Hobbes*
- O *Doonesbury*
- O *The Far Side*

125. *On the Revolutions of the Heavenly Spheres* is a 1543 book by which astronomer?

- O Galileo
- O Kepler
- O Copernicus

126. Margaret Thatcher's son Mark got lost while driving in which desert in 1982?

- O Sahara
- O Gobi
- O Atacama

127. The author Gerald Durrell established a zoo on which of the Channel Islands in the 1950s?

- O Jersey
- O Guernsey
- O Alderney

128. Who became the Queen of the Netherlands in 1980?

- O Benedicte
- O Bernadette
- O Beatrix

129. In Norse mythology, what type of creature is Fafnir?

- O Dragon
- O Giant
- O Dwarf

130. Ascorbic acid is an alternative name for which vitamin?

- O Vitamin A
- O Vitamin B
- O Vitamin C

131. The cricketer Brian Lara scored his record-breaking 501 not out against which English county side?

- O Yorkshire
- O Warwickshire
- O Durham

132. In the TV sitcom *Friends*, what is the name of Phoebe's identical twin sister?

- O Ursula
- O Gudrun
- O Hermione

133. Who played the role of Danny Zuko when *Grease* the musical was first performed in London?

- O Al Pacino
- O Christopher Walken
- O Richard Gere

134. What is the collective name for a group of tigers?

- O Trap
- O Ambush
- O Attack

135. The fictional character of Dracula was named after which historical figure?

- O Ivan the Terrible
- O Peter the Great
- O Vlad the Impaler

136. Which *Carry On* film regular was once a ladies' hairdresser in his native South Africa?

- O Charles Hawtrey
- O Sid James
- O Bernard Bresslaw

137. Which poet was a member of the pop group Scaffold?

- O Andrew Motion
- O Jon Hegley
- O Roger McGough

138. Before his retirement in August 2000, what was the profession of George Carman, a man often referred to as 'The Silver Fox'?

- O Architect
- O Doctor
- O Barrister

139. What is the literal meaning of the Afrikaans word 'boer'?

- O Farmer
- O Soldier
- O Traveller

140. Which female tennis player won eight Wimbledon singles titles between 1927 and 1938?

- O Maureen Connolly
- O Helen Wills Moody
- O Louise Brough

141. Which Italian region is known as the 'heel of Italy'?

- O Tuscany
- O Calabria
- O Puglia

142. What is the collective noun for a group of donkeys?

- O Dredge
- O Drove
- O Drizzle

143. Which English river flows through the town of Ipswich?

- O Orwell
- O Deben
- O Waveney

144. In 1999, the *Sun* newspaper printed pictures of Sophie Rhys-Jones cavorting with which TV presenter?

- O Johnny Vaughan
- O Nick Knowles
- O Chris Tarrant

145. Which actress starred in the 1927 film *It*, in the process becoming the world's first It girl?

- O Clara Bow
- O Carole Lombard
- O Lillian Gish

146. Princess Elizabeth, later to become Elizabeth II, was holidaying in which country when she heard the news that she had become Queen of England?

- O Kenya
- O Tanzania
- O South Africa

147. Who rode Red Rum to triumph in both the 1973 and 1974 Grand Nationals?

- O Tommy Carberry
- O Jonjo O'Neill
- O Brian Fletcher

148. Gilgamesh is a king and warrior from the mythology of which ancient civilisation?

- O Mesopotamia
- O Egypt
- O Aztec

149. When George W. Bush was arrested for driving under the influence of alcohol in 1976, which former Wimbledon champion was sitting in the passenger seat?

- O John Newcombe
- O Rod Laver
- O Roy Emerson

150. What number, referred to as 'le grande', do players attempt to score in the card game baccarat?

- O Twenty-five
- O Seventeen
- O Nine

KEVIN ASHMAN
Science

Full name:
Kevin Clifford Ashman

Home town:
Winchester

Education:
Degree in Modern History from Southampton University

Quizzing credentials:

2004–06	World Quizzing Champion
2004–06	European Quizzing Champion
2004–06	British Quizzing Champion
1996	*Brain of Britain*
1998	Brain of Brains
1998	Top Brain
1995	*Mastermind* Champion (specialist subject in the final – the Zulu War). Record score of forty-one achieved in the heats (specialist subject – Martin Luther King).
1995–6	Winner of *Masterbrain*

Strongest Eggheads subject:
Science

Least favourite subject:
Food and Drink

Interests:
History; visiting National Trust and English Heritage sites; World and European Cinema; Theatre; Classical concerts, and folk music.

Science

1. 'Cirrus' and 'nimbostratus' are examples of which type of weather phenomenon?

- *O* Cloud
- *O* Lightning
- *O* Sleet

2. In terms of astronomy, what is the Milky Way?

- *O* Galaxy
- *O* Meteor
- *O* Star

3. The semi-aquatic mammal, the platypus, is endemic to which country?

- *O* Brazil
- *O* Norway
- *O* Australia

4. What is the name of the small forms of plant and animal life that exist in the upper layers of the ocean?

- *O* Plankton
- *O* Kelp
- *O* Krill

5. Pb is the chemical symbol of which element?

- *O* Gold
- *O* Lead
- *O* Nitrogen

6. Which gland in the human body produces tears?

- *O* Apocrine
- *O* Thyroid
- *O* Lacrimal

7. After Jupiter, which is the largest planet in our solar system?

- O Mars
- O Saturn
- O Earth

8. By what collective name are the stars Castor and Pollux better known?

- O Gemini
- O Sagittarius
- O Aries

9. 'Mosquito Hawk' and 'Devil's Arrow' are alternative names for which insect?

- O Dragonfly
- O Stag Beetle
- O Bumble Bee

10. What is the technical term for short-sightedness?

- O Myopia
- O Dystopia
- O Meropia

11. The chemical process of 'desalination' is designed to remove which substance from water?

- O Salt
- O Sugar
- O Oxygen

12. What does the M stand for in the computer acronym ROM?

- O Memory
- O Modem
- O Mouse

13. In degrees Celsius, what is the boiling point of water?

O Zero

O Fifty

O One hundred

14. The goldfish is a small member of which fish family?

O Perch

O Pike

O Carp

15. Quicksilver is another name for which chemical element?

O Mercury

O Helium

O Gold

16. What type of acid is formed by milk that goes sour?

O Ascetic

O Lactic

O Ascorbic

17. 'Conical', 'shield' and 'hotspot' are examples of which type of geological phenomenon?

O Canyon

O Peninsula

O Volcano

18. Which metal is an alloy of copper and zinc?

O Steel

O Brass

O Platinum

19. In trigonometry, what term is ascribed to the longest side of a right-angled triangle?

- O Cosine
- O Tangent
- O Hypotenuse

20. The substance called Royal Jelly is produced by which creatures?

- O Bees
- O Wasps
- O Mosquitoes

21. The 'stapes' or 'stirrup' bone is located in which part of the human body?

- O Foot
- O Ear
- O Pelvis

22. Which computer company was founded by Steve Jobs and Steve Wozniak in the 1970s?

- O Microsoft
- O Amstrad
- O Apple

23. The precious stone diamond is composed of which non-metallic element?

- O Carbon
- O Silicon
- O Lead

24. What does the S stand for in the medical condition SAD?

- O Seasonal
- O Summer
- O Syndrome

25. In which year did Dr Christiaan Barnard perform the first human heart transplant?

- O 1947
- O 1957
- O 1967

26. The koala feeds chiefly on the leaves of which tree?

- O Bamboo
- O Jacaranda
- O Eucalyptus

27. Which early physician was referred to by Plato as 'the asclepiad of Cos'?

- O Hippocrates
- O Galen
- O Polybus

28. The condor bird is native to which continent?

- O South America
- O Africa
- O Asia

29. Which gas constitutes approximately 78 per cent of the Earth's atmosphere?

- O Nitrogen
- O Hydrogen
- O Helium

30. Which deadly virus, named after a river in Zaire, was first discovered in 1976?

- O Ebola virus
- O Epstein-Barr virus
- O Pogosta virus

31. What does the letter L represent in the scientific acronym LASER?

- O Light
- O Lithium
- O Laminate

32. In the natural world, what is a 'prickly pear'?

- O Cactus
- O Fungus
- O Nettle

33. Ergophobia is the scientific term for the irrational fear of what?

- O Latin
- O Yourself
- O Work

34. Which American scientist, born in 1847, patented over 1,000 inventions in his lifetime?

- O Thomas Edison
- O Eli Whitney
- O Benjamin Franklin

35. In biology, what name is given to the process by which water is transported into and out of cells?

- O Refraction
- O Evaporation
- O Osmosis

36. Carpal Tunnel Syndrome primarily affects which part of the human body?

- O Hands
- O Back
- O Eyes

37. What was the first name of Mr Nobel, the scientist and founder of the Nobel Prizes?

- O Jacques
- O Vladimir
- O Alfred

38. In mathematics, what does a figure of eight lying on its side represent?

- O Infinity
- O Intersection
- O Square root

39. The bonobo is a miniature variety of which animal?

- O Chimpanzee
- O Lion
- O Eagle

40. In our solar system, what is the third planet from the Sun?

- O Mercury
- O Saturn
- O Earth

41. Which infectious disease is spread by the female Anopheles mosquito?

- O Malaria
- O Dengue fever
- O Glandular fever

42. What type of animal is a 'springbok'?

- O Large cat
- O New World monkey
- O Antelope

43. Which hormone, responsible for regulating the level of glucose in the bloodstream, derives its name from the Latin word for 'island'?

- O Testosterone
- O Adrenalin
- O Insulin

44. Launched in 1957, what was the name of the first man-made, Earth-orbiting satellite?

- O *Vostok-1*
- O *Sputnik-1*
- O *Mir-1*

45. What type of creatures are 'cherry barbs' and 'neon tetras'?

- O Insects
- O Birds
- O Fish

46. Which liquid takes its name from the Latin words meaning 'rock' and 'oil'?

- O Petroleum
- O Gasoline
- O Paraffin

47. What species of shark is considered to be the largest fish in the world?

- O Whale shark
- O Great white shark
- O Hammerhead shark

48. What type of large gamefish, known to grow up to 2.5 metres long, has a spear-like snout and a high, rigid dorsal fin?

- O Marlin
- O Pike
- O Piranha

49. Entomology is the scientific study of which life forms?

- *O* Insects
- *O* Birds
- *O* Fish

50. Which chemical element, with the atomic number 12, burns with an intense white flame when ignited?

- *O* Sulphur
- *O* Potassium
- *O* Magnesium

51. What type of an animal is a 'Bombay duck'?

- *O* Bird
- *O* Fish
- *O* Insect

52. What name is given to the young of an elephant?

- *O* Foal
- *O* Pup
- *O* Calf

53. Phobos and Deimos are satellites of which planet?

- *O* Mars
- *O* Uranus
- *O* Neptune

54. What sort of creature would a lepidopterist study?

- *O* Butterflies
- *O* Birds
- *O* Beavers

55. Aspirin was originally derived from the bark of which type of tree?

- O Oak
- O Willow
- O Beech

56. 'To every action there is always opposed an equal reaction,' is a law of motion formulated by which scientist?

- O Isaac Newton
- O Stephen Hawking
- O Albert Einstein

57. Which fish is often referred to as 'the tiger of the sea' due to its ferocious nature?

- O Barracuda
- O Pike
- O Piranha

58. The illness diphtheria primarily affects which part of the human body?

- O Throat
- O Stomach
- O Eyes

59. Which disease common to children is a form of the 'varicella-zoster' virus?

- O Croup
- O Mumps
- O Chickenpox

60. Which species of bird became extinct on 3 July 1844, when the last two of their number were killed by hunters just off the coast of Iceland?

- O Great auk
- O Passenger pigeon
- O Elephant bird

61. Sleeping sickness is transmitted by which insect?

- *O* Tsetse fly
- *O* Jungle leech
- *O* Black rat

62. An apiculturist concerns himself with which type of animal?

- *O* Bees
- *O* Spiders
- *O* Beetles

63. What was the surname of the brothers named George and Laszlo, who invented the ballpoint pen in the 1930s?

- *O* Stylus
- *O* Bic
- *O* Biro

64. Which artery in the human body carries deoxygenated blood to the lungs?

- *O* Capillary
- *O* Thrombacic
- *O* Pulmonary

65. What type of bird is the roadrunner?

- *O* Cuckoo
- *O* Eagle
- *O* Magpie

66. The disease rickets is caused by a deficiency of which vitamin?

- *O* Vitamin A
- *O* Vitamin C
- *O* Vitamin D

67. Who was the first Briton in space?

- O Helen Sharman
- O Dennis Tito
- O Michael Foale

68. Igor Sikorsky is a pioneer of which type of transportation?

- O Helicopter
- O Motorbike
- O Aeroplane

69. What type of creature is the Australian 'drongo'?

- O Bird
- O Fish
- O Crocodile

70. What is the name of the condition that causes people who are held hostage to form strong, sympathetic bonds with their abductors?

- O Helsinki syndrome
- O Oslo syndrome
- O Stockholm syndrome

71. What is the name of the section of the Earth that lies between the crust and the central core of the planet?

- O Schism
- O Mantle
- O Earth shelf

72. Timothy Berners-Lee played a major role in the development of which scientific innovation?

- O Television
- O Car
- O Internet

73. An incision is made in which part of the human body in a tracheotomy operation?

- O Heart
- O Lung
- O Neck

74. Lockjaw is another name for which contagious disease?

- O Tetanus
- O Mumps
- O Measles

75. Sidewinders are examples of which type of snake?

- O Sea snake
- O Anaconda
- O Rattlesnake

76. The term 'vaccination' was first coined by which scientist?

- O Edward Jenner
- O Pierre Curie
- O Alexander Fleming

77. The deltoid muscles are in which part of the human body?

- O Shoulder
- O Arm
- O Lower back

78. The komodo dragon, the world's largest lizard, is native to which country?

- O Madagascar
- O Japan
- O Indonesia

79. Gynophobia is the irrational fear of what?

- O Women
- O Alcohol
- O Helicopters

80. The falabella is a miniature variety of which animal?

- O Horse
- O Dog
- O Cow

81. In 1947, who became the first pilot to break the sound barrier?

- O Gus Grissom
- O Scott Crossfield
- O Chuck Yeager

82. The otoscope is an instrument designed for the examination of which part of the human body?

- O Ear
- O Nose
- O Mouth

83. Dry ice is the solid form of which chemical compound?

- O Calcium hydroxide
- O Carbon dioxide
- O Hydrogen sulphate

84. In which marine creature does the male of the species carry the fertilized eggs?

- O Seahorse
- O Swordfish
- O Manatee

85. What is the technical name for the upper jawbone of the human skeleton?

- O Mandible
- O Maxilla
- O Radial

86. The word 'nephritic' refers specifically to which organ of the human body?

- O Kidneys
- O Heart
- O Liver

87. In astronomy, 'elliptical', 'spiral' and 'irregular' are all varieties of what?

- O Galaxy
- O Wormhole
- O Planet

88. The 'sea wasp' is an alternative name for which creature?

- O Barracuda
- O Manta Ray
- O Jellyfish

89. What was the name of the car in which Andy Green broke the land speed record in 1997?

- O *Force SSC*
- O *Thrust SSC*
- O *Torque SSC*

90. What SI unit of power is equal to one joule of work performed per second?

- O Hertz
- O Ohm
- O Watt

91. Which animal takes its name from the Malaysian word meaning 'man of the forest'?

- O Orang-utan
- O Gorilla
- O Baboon

92. What name is given to the scientific study of the causes and nature of disease?

- O Oncology
- O Pathology
- O Toxicology

93. What is the name of the flashes of atmospheric electricity that often appear above a ship's mast during stormy weather?

- O St Elmo's Fire
- O Will o' the Wisp
- O Baily's Beads

94. Which supercontinent, whose name was taken from the Greek for 'all earth', incorporated all dry land on Earth until its break up over 200 million years ago?

- O Pangaea
- O Lorentia
- O Khanty

95. In which year did Halley's Comet last pass by the Sun and Earth?

- O 1976
- O 1986
- O 1996

96. What is the medical term for the sleep disorder known as 'teeth grinding'?

- O Epistaxis
- O Bruxism
- O Pyrosis

97. In 1952, Jonas Salk developed the first successful vaccine for which disease?

- Polio
- Smallpox
- Leprosy

98. What type of flower is a 'Lady's Slipper'?

- Orchid
- Rhododendron
- Azalia

99. Which of these is one of the four 'humours' identified by the early Greek physician Hippocrates?

- Phlegm
- Adrenalin
- Marrow

100. Who was the first American astronaut in space?

- Jim Lovell
- Alan Shepard
- Neil Armstrong

101. The aurochs is an extinct species of which animal?

- Tiger
- Cow
- Eagle

102. Of what is 'petrology' the study?

- Rocks
- Shells
- Teeth

103. What is another name for the thrombocytes in the human blood that stick together to form clots when the skin is broken?

- O Plasma
- O White blood cells
- O Platelets

104. The 'spectacled bear' is native to which of the world's mountain ranges?

- O Andes
- O Himalayas
- O Alps

105. What was the first name of the astronomer after whom the Hubble telescope was named?

- O Lyndon
- O Ralph
- O Edwin

106. Sternutation is another name for which human reflex?

- O Sneezing
- O Blinking
- O Laughing

107. What is an 'angiosperm'?

- O A hoofed mammal
- O A flowering plant
- O A flesh-eating virus

108. The BCG vaccine guards against which disease?

- O Tuberculosis
- O Polio
- O Rubella

109. The mathematical term 'algebra' comes from which language?

- O Hindi
- O Yiddish
- O Arabic

110. What was the first name of the man who invented Morse code?

- O Simon
- O Samuel
- O Seamus

111. Before its extinction, the dodo bird was native to which island?

- O Cuba
- O Mauritius
- O Tahiti

112. The Fields Medal is a prestigious award given out for excellence in which field of endeavour?

- O Astrophysics
- O Quantum mechanics
- O Mathematics

113. Who was the first woman to win the Nobel Prize for Physics?

- O Marie Curie
- O Rosalind Franklin
- O Stephanie Kwolek

114. Emma Wedgwood was the wife of which scientist?

- O Isaac Newton
- O Charles Darwin
- O Thomas Edison

115. How many pairs of chromosomes are there in a normal human cell?

- *O* Twenty-three
- *O* Forty-three
- *O* Sixty-three

116. By what name is the brontosaurus dinosaur also known?

- *O* Apatosaurus
- *O* Diplodocus
- *O* Brachiosaurus

117. What does an 'anemometer' measure?

- *O* Temperature
- *O* Rainfall
- *O* Wind speed

118. What would you be doing if you were suffering from a transient form of the condition 'erythema'?

- *O* Blushing
- *O* Fainting
- *O* Sleeping

119. By what two-word name is 'laughing gas' also known?

- *O* Nitrous oxide
- *O* Calcium oxide
- *O* Hydrogen oxide

120. The tarantula spider is named after a town in which country?

- *O* Mexico
- *O* Spain
- *O* Italy

121. What does the word 'planet' mean when translated from the Greek?

- *O* Bauble
- *O* Wanderer
- *O* Giant

122. Which Ancient mathematician reputedly defended the city of Syracuse by inventing war machines that sank the ships of the attackers?

- *O* Copernicus
- *O* Pythagoras
- *O* Archimedes

123. Which theoretical shortcut between two points in space is referred to as an 'Einstein-Rosen bridge'?

- *O* Black hole
- *O* Wormhole
- *O* Time loop

124. What is the name of the disputed tenth planet in our solar system, discovered in March 2004?

- *O* Circe
- *O* Freya
- *O* Sedna

125. What type of acid is commonly found in tea and wood-stain?

- *O* Tannic acid
- *O* Sorbic acid
- *O* Malic acid

126. Who was the first US astronaut to complete an orbit of the Earth?

- *O* John Glenn
- *O* Jack Swigert
- *O* Buzz Aldrin

127. Gregor Mendel was a pioneer in which field of science?

- O Genetics
- O IVF
- O Transplant surgery

128. Which physicist, born in 1635, is best known for discovering the Law of Elasticity that bears his name?

- O Wilhelm Roentgen
- O Michael Faraday
- O Robert Hooke

129. The 'tetralogy of Fallot' is a congenital condition that specifically affects which organ of the human body?

- O Heart
- O Liver
- O Brain

130. 'Work expands to fill the time allotted for its completion,' is a psychological law devised by which writer?

- O Frederick Soddy
- O Edward Murphy
- O Cyril Parkinson

131. The 'great red spot' is a feature of which planet in our solar system?

- O Jupiter
- O Pluto
- O Mars

132. Which chemical element was named after the Greek word for 'lazy' due to its inert nature?

- O Argon
- O Mercury
- O Lead

133. Leonids and Perseids are examples of which astrological phenomenon?

- *O* Solar flare
- *O* Total solar eclipse
- *O* Meteor shower

134. Which scientist successfully used carbolic acid as a surgical antiseptic for the first time in 1865?

- *O* Robert Hamilton Russell
- *O* William Harvey
- *O* Joseph Lister

135. What is the brightest star in the night sky?

- *O* Vega
- *O* Rigel
- *O* Sirius

136. What is the name of the smallest species of penguin in the world?

- *O* Dwarf penguin
- *O* Elf penguin
- *O* Fairy penguin

137. Who won the 1903 Nobel Prize for Physics and the 1911 Nobel Prize for Chemistry?

- *O* Marie Curie
- *O* Albert Einstein
- *O* Nikolas Tesla

138. Which thirteenth-century scientist and monk was known as Doctor Mirabilis?

- *O* Roger Bacon
- *O* Nostradamus
- *O* Andreas Vesalius

139. What type of fish is an albacore?

- O Tuna
- O Herring
- O Pike

140. Which scientist, born in 1822, developed the world's first successful vaccine for rabies?

- O Edward Jenner
- O Louis Pasteur
- O Pierre Curie

141. What is the world's largest venomous snake?

- O King cobra
- O Black mamba
- O Mexican rattlesnake

142. Which planet was discovered by Clyde Tombaugh in 1930?

- O Mars
- O Saturn
- O Pluto

143. What type of bird is the kea, known for its tendency to hunt sheep?

- O Budgerigar
- O Thrush
- O Parrot

144. Which gas gives Uranus its distinctive blue-green colouring?

- O Methane
- O Chlorine
- O Helium

145. What is the main irritant in the leaves of a stinging nettle?

- O Nitric acid
- O Formic acid
- O Lactic acid

146. What metal conducts electricity better than any other?

- O Silver
- O Gold
- O Platinum

147. Which element in the periodic table takes its name from the German for 'evil spirit'?

- O Bromine
- O Sulphur
- O Cobalt

148. Vitamin B2 is better known by what name?

- O Riboflavin
- O Oil of vitriol
- O Retinol

149. What is the name of the theoretical opposite of the Big Bang?

- O Big Crunch
- O Big Squeeze
- O Big Shrink

150. What is the name of the process by which food is passed through the human intestine?

- O Pericarp
- O Pericycle
- O Peristalsis

Answers on p.291

General Knowledge

1. What is the meaning of the German word 'Kinder'?

- *O* School
- *O* Teacher
- *O* Children

2. What does the P stand for in the banking acronym PIN number?

- *O* Personal
- *O* Punch
- *O* Public

3. In the game of Bingo, what is the traditional call for the number one?

- *O* Kelly's Eye
- *O* Man Alive
- *O* Red Raw

4. What type of animal was Sylvester in the Warner Brothers cartoons?

- *O* Rooster
- *O* Mouse
- *O* Cat

5. What is the name of the type of strong brown paper that is named after an Asian capital city?

- *O* Jakarta paper
- *O* Hanoi paper
- *O* Manila paper

6. In the nursery rhyme 'Pop Goes The Weasel', what sort of rice is bought?

- *O* Halfpenny rice
- *O* Tuppenny rice
- *O* Thruppenny rice

7. The last total eclipse of the Sun visible in the UK occurred in which year?

- O 1999
- O 1969
- O 1939

8. Which board game takes its name from the Latin word meaning 'I play'?

- O Risk
- O Mah Jong
- O Ludo

9. Acapulco is a tourist resort in which country?

- O Colombia
- O Mexico
- O Belize

10. In terms of area, what is the largest US state?

- O Rhode Island
- O Alabama
- O Alaska

11. Steve Harmison represents England in which sport?

- O Tennis
- O Football
- O Cricket

12. Stud and Texas Hold 'Em are varieties of which card game?

- O Poker
- O Baccarat
- O Bridge

13. Which Lieutenant Colonel and NSC staff member admitted selling arms to Iran to fund the anti-Marxist Nicaraguan Contra rebels in the 1980s?

- O Oliver North
- O Donald Rumsfeld
- O Norman Schwarzkopf

14. *Rockney* and *Don't Give A Monkey's* are titles of albums by which musical act?

- O Chas and Dave
- O Blur
- O Babyshambles

15. Which day of the week is named after the hammer-wielding Norse god of thunder?

- O Wednesday
- O Thursday
- O Friday

16. Queen Gertrude and King Claudius are characters in which Shakespeare play?

- O *Macbeth*
- O *Othello*
- O *Hamlet*

17. In which year did Eddie 'the Eagle' Edwards represent Great Britain in the Olympic Games?

- O 1980
- O 1988
- O 1996

18. People who suffer from chromophobia suffer from an irrational fear of what?

- O Colours
- O Sound
- O Water

19. In which decade did ITV begin broadcasting?

- O 1930s
- O 1950s
- O 1970s

20. The seeds of which species of tree are known as 'conkers'?

- O Cedar
- O Sycamore
- O Horse chestnut

21. What are traditionally used in the gambling game Craps?

- O Dice
- O Cards
- O Marbles

22. Peter Glaze, Ed Stewart and Stu Francis were presenters of which long-running children's TV show?

- O *Jackanory*
- O *Blue Peter*
- O *Crackerjack*

23. Reed Richards and The Thing are members of which superhero team, created by Stan Lee and Jack Kirby in 1961?

- O The Avengers
- O The X-Men
- O The Fantastic Four

24. Annie Leibowitz is a leading figure in which branch of the arts?

- O Sculpture
- O Photography
- O Ballet

25. The word 'tor' is a Celtic term for which type of geographical feature?

- O Hill
- O Valley
- O Lake

26. Which British city contains an area of curry restaurants known as 'the Balti Belt'?

- O Norwich
- O Swansea
- O Birmingham

27. Uther Pendragon was the father of which legendary figure?

- O King Arthur
- O Beowulf
- O Siegfried

28. Before becoming a full-time actor, Harrison Ford worked in what field?

- O Plumbing
- O Masonry
- O Carpentry

29. 'Horseshoe', 'cascade' and 'punchbowl' are types of which geographical feature?

- O Waterfall
- O Ravine
- O Glacier

30. Traditionally, what does a farrier make?

- O Barrels
- O Gloves
- O Horseshoes

31. What type of cheese takes its name from the Italian for 'sweet milk'?

O Pecorino

O Dolcelatte

O Parmesan

32. By what name was Henry Cooper's celebrated left hook better known?

O 'Enery's 'Ammer

O 'Enery's Welly

O 'Enery's Clout

33. What does the C stand for in the name of the CBE award?

O Commander

O Chief

O Captain

34. In Greek mythology, who devised the plan of the 'Trojan horse'?

O Heracles

O Theseus

O Odysseus

35. According to Irish folklore, which items are made by leprechauns?

O Shoes

O Flutes

O Necklaces

36. By what name is the game of Noughts and Crosses also known?

O Tikal

O Tic-Tac-Toe

O Tric-Trac

37. In which sport could competitors use a 'spider' and a 'half-butt'?

- O Fencing
- O Squash
- O Snooker

38. The seaside town of Whitstable is most commonly associated with which type of seafood?

- O Oysters
- O Lobsters
- O Prawns

39. What was the name of the secret system that was set up in America to help slaves escape the southern states before the Act of Emancipation?

- O Underground steamship
- O Underground railroad
- O Underground stagecoach

40. 'I was exceedingly surprised with the print of a man's naked foot on the shore,' is a line from which 1719 novel?

- O *Robinson Crusoe*
- O *Treasure Island*
- O *Kidnapped!*

41. In nineteenth-century Britain, what were 'peelers'?

- O Bankers
- O Policemen
- O Doctors

42. Which herbivorous dinosaur takes its name from the Greek for 'roof lizard'?

- O Velociraptor
- O Stegosaurus
- O Diplodocus

43. Barristers who have achieved the rank of QC are often known by what informal term?

- O Cottons
- O Satins
- O Silks

44. The Tyrol is a region of which mountain range?

- O Andes
- O Alps
- O Caucasus

45. Which Olympic gold medal-winning former athlete was the MP for Falmouth and Cambourne between 1992 and 1997?

- O Linford Christie
- O Sebastian Coe
- O Steve Ovett

46. Johnny Weissmuller, famous for portraying Tarzan in several films of the 1930s and 1940s, won five Olympic gold medals in which sport?

- O Athletics
- O Swimming
- O Equestrianism

47. The Cresta Run is a celebrated venue in which sport?

- O Bobsled
- O Horse Racing
- O Formula 1

48. 'To die will be an awfully big adventure,' is a line from which work of the early twentieth century?

- O *The Hobbit*
- O *The Wind in the Willows*
- O *Peter Pan*

49. What instrument does Charlie Watts play in the Rolling Stones?

O Drums

O Bass guitar

O Harmonica

50. Slash was the lead guitarist for which rock group?

O Poison

O Guns 'n' Roses

O Aerosmith

51. Which comedian was famously said to have had 'short, fat, hairy legs'?

O Ernie Wise

O Bob Monkhouse

O Harry Worth

52. In Greek mythology, what was the name of the many-headed serpent destroyed by Heracles?

O Cerberus

O Hydra

O Chimera

53. Whom did Sven-Göran Eriksson succeed as the official manager of the England football team?

O Glenn Hoddle

O Terry Venables

O Kevin Keegan

54. Mike Skinner is the songwriter and musician behind which musical act?

O The Streets

O So Solid Crew

O Blazin' Squad

55. In which nursery rhyme does a shepherd boy sleep under a haystack?

- Little Boy Blue
- Three Blind Mice
- Little Jack Horner

56. William Luther Robinson, better known as Mr Bojangles, was a leading exponent of which type of dancing?

- Tango
- Tap
- Flamenco

57. The song 'There's No Business Like Show Business' comes from which Irving Berlin musical?

- *Annie Get Your Gun*
- *Top Hat*
- *Holiday Inn*

58. Which fictional character was created by Mary Tourtel?

- Tarzan
- Rupert the Bear
- Tarka the Otter

59. What type of vehicle is a 'felucca'?

- Glider
- Moped
- Boat

60. *The English Roses* is the title of a children's book by which singer?

- Beyoncé Knowles
- Madonna
- Geri Halliwell

61. Which character in *The Avengers* was played by Honor Blackman?

- O Cathy Gale
- O Tara King
- O Emma Peel

62. Which rider, born in 1904, won the title of Champion Jockey a record twenty-six times?

- O Lester Piggott
- O Gordon Richards
- O Fred Archer

63. Who played the role of Vyvyan in the 1980s TV comedy *The Young Ones*?

- O Ade Edmonson
- O Rik Mayall
- O Nigel Planer

64. *Pet Sounds* is an influential album by which group?

- O The Mamas and the Papas
- O The Beach Boys
- O The Byrds

65. The ventriloquist Roger de Courcey is best known for his association with which puppet?

- O Spit the Dog
- O Cuddles the Monkey
- O Nookie Bear

66. Elvis Presley was born in which state in 1935?

- O Iowa
- O Florida
- O Mississippi

67. 'Men seldom make passes at girls who wear glasses,' is a quotation by which writer and wit?

- O Oscar Wilde
- O Dorothy Parker
- O Noël Coward

68. In 1812, who became the first British prime minister to be assassinated?

- O Pitt the Elder
- O Lord Salisbury
- O Spencer Perceval

69. The violinist Nigel Kennedy is a fan of which Premier League football team?

- O Aston Villa
- O Birmingham City
- O Leicester City

70. Who bought Jumbo the elephant from London Zoo in 1882?

- O Frederick Treves
- O Queen Victoria
- O P. T. Barnum

71. Which German footballer, born in 1945, was nicknamed 'The Kaiser'?

- O Jürgen Klinsman
- O Gerd Muller
- O Franz Beckenbauer

72. 'Here In My Heart', the first ever Number 1 in the official British charts, was recorded by which singer?

- O Al Martino
- O Bobby Darin
- O Tony Bennett

73. Which actor, born in 1883, was known as 'The Man of a Thousand Faces' because of his skill with make-up and disguise?

- O Errol Flynn
- O Peter Lorre
- O Lon Chaney

74. In music, what is the technical term for half of a note?

- O Breve
- O Minim
- O Crotchet

75. By what name is the radio presenter Marc Riley better known?

- O Lard
- O DJ Spoony
- O Rob da Bank

76. Which district of Paris is the highest point of the city and is dominated by the basilica of Sacré Coeur?

- O Montmartre
- O Montparnasse
- O Ile de la Cité

77. Who is said to have given the silent comedian Joseph Francis Keaton the nickname 'Buster'?

- O Harry Houdini
- O Charlie Chaplin
- O Sarah Bernhardt

78. In which country was the mountaineer Sir Edmund Hillary born?

- O Australia
- O Canada
- O New Zealand

79. Dale Arden was the girlfriend of which fictional hero?

- O Buck Rogers
- O Dick Tracy
- O Flash Gordon

80. The Chrysanthemum Throne is a historical term used to describe the ruler of which country?

- O Japan
- O Persia
- O Greece

81. Which boxer was known as 'The Clones Cyclone'?

- O Barry McGuigan
- O Lloyd Honeyghan
- O Alan Minter

82. In which 1960 film does Shirley Maclaine play the role of elevator operator Fran Kubelik?

- O *Some Like It Hot*
- O *Irma La Douce*
- O *The Apartment*

83. Which animals travel in 'mobs' under the leadership of a dominant male known as an 'old man' or a 'boomer'?

- O Kangaroos
- O Gorillas
- O Grizzly Bears

84. Which island group were referred to as The Seven Sisters by Portuguese explorers?

- O The Philippines
- O The Seychelles
- O The Dodecanese

85. Which of the Queen's sons did not attend university?

O Prince Charles

O Prince Andrew

O Prince Edward

86. The reality TV show *Big Brother* was first produced in which European country?

O Hungary

O Netherlands

O Germany

87. Which character from Greek mythology became so jealous of his nephew's skill as an inventor that he attempted to murder him?

O Actaeon

O Tantalus

O Daedalus

88. What was the name of Vincent Van Gogh's brother, with whom he shared a detailed correspondence until his death?

O Thierry

O Thomas

O Theo

89. The 1994 film *Quiz Show* examined corruption behind the scenes of which TV show in the 1960s?

O *Twenty-One*

O *Jeopardy*

O *The Price Is Right*

90. 'We didn't land on Plymouth Rock, my brothers and sisters. Plymouth Rock landed on us,' is a quotation by which public figure, born in 1925?

O Bobby Seale

O Malcolm X

O Martin Luther King

91. Mademoiselle Varenka and Count Vronsky are characters in which 1877 novel?

- O *War and Peace*
- O *Eugene Onegin*
- O *Anna Karenina*

92. Which hockey player was Great Britain's top scorer at the 1988 Olympics when they won a gold medal in the men's division?

- O Sean Bachelor
- O Imran Sherwani
- O Sean Kerly

93. By what name is the rutabaga vegetable also known?

- O Cucumber
- O Swede
- O Carrot

94. In 1971, who became the first man to turn down a Best Actor Oscar?

- O George C. Scott
- O Jack Nicholson
- O Robert De Niro

95. Which Tom Cruise film is a remake of the 1997 Spanish movie *Open Your Eyes*?

- O *Vanilla Sky*
- O *The Last Samurai*
- O *Jerry Maguire*

96. 'Minnie The Moocher' was the trademark piece of which American singer and jazz bandleader?

- O Cab Calloway
- O Chet Baker
- O Nina Simone

97. Which actor and comedian, born in 1935, was awarded a scholarship to study the organ at Magdalen College, Oxford?

- O Les Dawson
- O Hugh Laurie
- O Dudley Moore

98. 'Taikonaut' is a term for an astronaut from which country?

- O China
- O Japan
- O Russia

99. Though originating in Africa, the mysterious Voodoo religion is now based on which Caribbean country?

- O Haiti
- O Cuba
- O Tobago

100. 'The Blue Boy' is a 1770 painting by which artist?

- O Stubbs
- O Gainsborough
- O Turner

101. What was the real name of the American serial killer called 'the Son of Sam'?

- O David Berkowitz
- O John Wayne Gacy
- O Ted Bundy

102. Which award-winning TV series was created by David Chase?

- O *24*
- O *The Sopranos*
- O *Desperate Housewives*

103. In 1979, Mohammed Al-Fayed bought which Parisian hotel?

- O The Ritz
- O The Dorchester
- O The Savoy

104. What does a deltiologist collect?

- O Stamps
- O Beer mats
- O Postcards

105. CH is the international car index mark of which country?

- O Switzerland
- O Sweden
- O Spain

106. In 1987, which US politician saw his chances of becoming US president disappear after details of his affair with the model Donna Rice became public?

- O Gary Hart
- O Ross Perot
- O Michael Dukakis

107. Which hybrid berry is a cross between a raspberry and a blackberry?

- O Boysenberry
- O Loganberry
- O Blueberry

108. Who became the mayor of Cincinnati in 1977?

- O David Letterman
- O Montel Williams
- O Jerry Springer

109. George Hepplewhite is famed for making which product in the eighteenth century?

- O Clothes
- O Furniture
- O Pottery

110. Kabbalah is an offshoot of which religion?

- O Judaism
- O Buddhism
- O Hinduism

111. Which radio show, first broadcast on 22 December 1967, features a theme tune by Frederic Chopin?

- O *Just a Minute*
- O *Dead Ringers*
- O *Poetry Please*

112. In Greek mythology, who was the god of prophecy, music, poetry and healing?

- O Apollo
- O Hermes
- O Ares

113. The flag of which country depicts an eagle eating a snake?

- O Paraguay
- O Mexico
- O Egypt

114. The Iron Maiden singer Bruce Dickinson has represented England in which sport?

- O Fencing
- O Show jumping
- O Polo

115. Which early blues guitarist is reputed to have sold his soul to the devil at the crossroads in return for musical genius?

- O Muddy Waters
- O B. B. King
- O Robert Johnson

116. Wellington and Boot are characters in which comic strip by Dennis Collins?

- O *Calvin and Hobbes*
- O *The Perishers*
- O *Andy Capp*

117. What type of weapon was the 'pilum' as used by the armies of the Roman empire?

- O Spear
- O Axe
- O Sword

118. What is the lowest of all female singing voices?

- O Baritone
- O Bass
- O Contralto

119. The Ashmolean Museum is located in which British city?

- O Oxford
- O Cambridge
- O St Andrews

120. The Gypsy and Tiger Moth biplanes were designed by which aircraft company?

- O Sopwith
- O De Havilland
- O Gloster

121. Used for measuring horses, how many inches are there in a 'hand'?

- O Four
- O Ten
- O Fourteen

122. Which author came up with the famous advertising slogan, 'Go to work on an egg'?

- O Murray Walker
- O Germaine Greer
- O Fay Weldon

123. In 1966, Prince Charles became an exchange student to which country?

- O Australia
- O Canada
- O South Africa

124. What was the nickname of the great Welsh footballer John Charles?

- O The Long Fella
- O The Newport Tower
- O The Gentle Giant

125. Who played the role of Buck Barrow in the 1967 film *Bonnie and Clyde*?

- O Gene Hackman
- O Dustin Hoffman
- O Peter Boyle

126. Before it was converted into an art gallery, what was the Musée d'Orsay in Paris?

- O University
- O Royal palace
- O Railway station

127. In which year did Karol Jozef Wojtyla become Pope John Paul II?

- *O* 1968
- *O* 1978
- *O* 1988

128. Who played the role of the doomed Jeff Markham in the 1946 film noir *Out of the Past*?

- *O* Humphrey Bogart
- *O* Robert Mitchum
- *O* Kirk Douglas

129. Which actor played the role of J. Edgar Hoover in the 1995 film *Nixon*?

- *O* Bob Hoskins
- *O* Gary Oldman
- *O* Anthony Hopkins

130. *The Marriage of Heaven and Hell* is a prophetic eighteenth-century book by which writer and artist?

- *O* William Blake
- *O* Leonardo Da Vinci
- *O* Caravaggio

131. Which architect designed the Guggenheim Museum in Bilbao?

- *O* Frank Lloyd Wright
- *O* Frank Gehry
- *O* Antonio Gaudi

132. A destructive fire broke out in which London landmark on 16 October 1834?

- *O* Buckingham Palace
- *O* Houses of Parliament
- *O* The National Gallery

133. W. F. Deedes became the editor of which newspaper in 1974?

- O *Daily Mail*
- O *Guardian*
- O *Daily Telegraph*

134. The revolutionary leader Bernardo O'Higgins was the first head of state of which country?

- O Panama
- O Bolivia
- O Chile

135. George W. Bush passed out after choking on which foodstuff in January 2002?

- O Peanut
- O Pretzel
- O Freedom Fry

136. Which popular entertainer suggested that his epitaph should be, 'He was an average guy who could carry a tune'?

- O Bing Crosby
- O Frank Sinatra
- O Rudy Vallee

137. 'Getting To Know You' is a song from which stage musical?

- O *South Pacific*
- O *The King and I*
- O *On the Town*

138. Chuck D. and Flavor Flav are former members of which rap group?

- O NWA
- O De La Soul
- O Public Enemy

139. Which British boxer sensationally beat Sugar Ray Robinson on 10 July 1951?

- O Randolph Turpin
- O Ted 'Kid' Lewis
- O Benny Lynch

140. Which poet, born in August 1922, turned down the opportunity to succeed John Betjeman as Poet Laureate?

- O Stephen Spender
- O Thom Gunn
- O Philip Larkin

141. The diamond called the 'Great Star of Africa' is set in which element of the Crown Jewels?

- O Crown
- O Sword
- O Sceptre

142. Which coach masterminded the British Lions' victorious rugby union tour to New Zealand in 1971?

- O Carwyn James
- O Cliff Morgan
- O Dick Greenwood

143. First published in 1702, what was the name of Britain's first national daily newspaper?

- O *Daily Courant*
- O *Daily Register*
- O *Daily Announcements*

144. What was the official name of the Penny Farthing bicycle?

- O Normal Bicycle
- O Standard Bicycle
- O Ordinary Bicycle

145. In 1906, which country became the first in Europe to give votes to women?

- O Iceland
- O Finland
- O Italy

146. Who played the title role in the 1975 Stanley Kubrick film *Barry Lyndon*?

- O Albert Finney
- O Al Pacino
- O Ryan O'Neal

147. What was the name of the *Blue Peter* tortoise who sadly died in 2004 after twenty-two years on the show?

- O George
- O Gerald
- O Geoffrey

148. Which Greek dramatist was reputedly killed in 456BC when a passing eagle dropped a tortoise on his head?

- O Euripides
- O Aeschylus
- O Sophocles

149. 'Dee-dars' is a term occasionally used to describe people from which city?

- O Bradford
- O Leicester
- O Sheffield

150. What was the first name of Mr Cruft, the founder of the prestigious annual dog show?

- O Charles
- O Henry
- O Lionel

CHRIS HUGHES History

Full name:
Christopher John Hughes

Home town:
Born in Barnet, North London, Chris now lives in Crewe.

Education:
Chris was expelled from grammar school in Enfield at the age of fifteen. He went on to Tottenham Technical College where he gained four O levels in Maths, English, Chemistry and Physics.

Quizzing credentials:

1972 Won £100 on *The Sky's the Limit*

1982 *Top of the World*

1983 Mastermind Champion (specialist subject in the heats and final: British Steam Locomotives 1900–68.)

1983 *International Mastermind* Champion (Chris is the reigning champion, as this competition has not been held since).

Strongest Eggheads subject:
History

Least favourite subject:
Sport

Special interest:
Railways, technology, and obsolete transport.

Hobbies:
Amateur dramatics. Chris once played Bottom in *A Midsummer Night's Dream* back in 1971.

History

1. Who led a rebellion of slaves and gladiators against Rome in the Third Servile War during the first century BC?

- *O* Caracalla
- *O* Spartacus
- *O* Cicero

2. Which US president delivered the Gettysburg Address?

- *O* Abraham Lincoln
- *O* George Washington
- *O* Thomas Jefferson

3. What was the name of the German dirigible that caught fire on 6 May 1937 over Lakehurst Naval Station, New Jersey?

- *O* *Bismarck*
- *O* *Mayerling*
- *O* *Hindenburg*

4. Which military leader was known as either 'The Corsican' or 'The Little Corporal'?

- *O* Charles de Gaulle
- *O* Joan of Arc
- *O* Napoleon Bonaparte

5. The towns of Pompeii and Herculaneum was destroyed by the eruption of which volcano in AD79?

- *O* Etna
- *O* Vesuvius
- *O* Stromboli

6. Who said, 'Doctor Livingstone, I presume?' upon finally locating the elusive missionary in 1871?

- *O* Henry Morton Stanley
- *O* Richard Burton
- *O* Mungo Park

7. Which gambler and outlaw fought alongside Wyatt Earp in the Gunfight at the OK Corral?

- O Billy the Kid
- O Butch Cassidy
- O Doc Holliday

8. Which criminal made a daring escape from Wandsworth Prison in 1965 before fleeing to France, Australia and, finally, Brazil?

- O Ronnie Biggs
- O Buster Edwards
- O Ronnie Kray

9. Which English king is reputed to have allowed cakes to burn on the stove, so preoccupied was he by the state of the nation?

- O Alfred the Great
- O Ethelred the Unready
- O Richard the Lionheart

10. In which year was India granted independence from Great Britain?

- O 1887
- O 1947
- O 1977

11. What was the surname of the US senator who was the driving force behind the Communist witch-hunts of the 1950s?

- O McKinley
- O McCarthy
- O McKenzie

12. What is the name of the code machine used by the Germans during the Second World War?

- *O* Riddle
- *O* Enigma
- *O* Puzzle

13. Which town gave its name to the puppet government, headed by Philippe Pétain, that was set up by the Germans in France during the Second World War?

- *O* Vichy
- *O* Sauternes
- *O* Poitiers

14. Until 1943, which island at the mouth of the Hudson River was the main processing station for immigrants wishing to live in New York?

- *O* Liberty Island
- *O* Ellis Island
- *O* Long Island

15. Who said, 'I believe it is peace for our time', on 30 September 1938?

- *O* Clement Attlee
- *O* Stanley Baldwin
- *O* Neville Chamberlain

16. In 1849, thousands of prospectors arrived in which American state in the hope of finding gold?

- *O* Oregon
- *O* California
- *O* Florida

17. Which historical figure was known as 'The Nine Days' Queen'?

- *O* Anne Boleyn
- *O* Lady Jane Grey
- *O* Mary, Queen of Scots

18. Which English king was forced to grant the Magna Carta in 1215?

O John

O Richard I

O Edward I

19. Which British military leader is said to have refused to do battle with the Spanish until he had finished his game of bowls?

O Drake

O Raleigh

O Cochrane

20. The treaty that formally ended the Second World War was signed in which French building?

O The Louvre

O The Palace of Versailles

O Notre Dame Cathedral

21. Mata Hari was executed on charges of espionage during which war?

O First World War

O Second World War

O Korean War

22. What was the name of the last imperial Russian dynasty?

O Bourbon

O Savoy

O Romanov

23. Which country did Garibaldi fight to unify in the nineteenth century?

O Italy

O Germany

O Turkey

24. In which year did the *Titanic* sink?

- O 1912
- O 1924
- O 1936

25. Against which country did England wage the Hundred Years' War?

- O Germany
- O Italy
- O France

26. In medieval Japan, what were 'ronin'?

- O Tradesmen
- O Geishas
- O Samurai

27. The Grimaldis have been the ruling family of which state since 1297?

- O Monaco
- O Andorra
- O San Marino

28. What was the name of the summer palace of the Mongol emperor Kublai Khan?

- O Shangri-La
- O Utopia
- O Xanadu

29. What nickname was given to the troops trained by Oliver Cromwell during the English Civil War?

- O Blockheads
- O Ironsides
- O Leatherjackets

30. St Paul's Cathedral was rebuilt in the seventeenth century to the designs of which architect?

- O John Nash
- O Christopher Wren
- O John Caius

31. In which war did the British Army use tanks for the first time?

- O Second World War
- O Crimean War
- O First World War

32. The English king William the Conqueror was also the duke of which region of France?

- O Normandy
- O Brittany
- O Alsace

33. The Boston Tea Party of 1773 precipitated which major conflict?

- O American Civil War
- O American Revolution
- O First World War

34. Who appeared on the First World War armed services recruitment poster bearing the slogan, 'Your country needs you!'?

- O Haig
- O Baden-Powell
- O Kitchener

35. Which country declared war on Germany in 1917?

- O USA
- O Russia
- O Japan

36. David Ben-Gurion was the first prime minister of which country?

- O Israel
- O Egypt
- O Iran

37. Juan Domingo Péron became president of which country in 1946?

- O Argentina
- O Brazil
- O Chile

38. What nickname did the British give to the V-1 flying bomb during the Second World War?

- O Fiddlebug
- O Doodlebug
- O Beedlebug

39. From 1696 to 1851, the British government levied a tax on which part of a house?

- O Toilets
- O Doors
- O Windows

40. In which century was Charles I of England executed?

- O Fifteenth
- O Sixteenth
- O Seventeenth

41. Where did the American hero Jim Bowie die?

- O The Alamo
- O Bunker Hill
- O Pearl Harbor

42. Which historical figure was known as 'Temujin'?

- O Attila the Hun
- O Tamburlaine
- O Genghis Khan

43. What name was given to members of the militia who served on the American side during the US War of Independence?

- O Secondmen
- O Minutemen
- O Hourmen

44. Who were the praetorian guard supposed to protect?

- O Roman emperors
- O Egyptian pharaohs
- O US presidents

45. On 17 November 1603, which naval hero and explorer was put on trial for treason for his part in the 'main plot' to remove James I from the throne?

- O James Wolfe
- O Thomas Cochrane
- O Walter Raleigh

46. Which historical battle was partially fought on Senlac Hill?

- O Hastings
- O Agincourt
- O Crécy

47. A man named Stakhanov, who set famous productivity records and was referred to by the authorities as 'the model Soviet worker', operated in which industry?

- O Steel working
- O Car making
- O Coal mining

48. Which German soldier of the Second World War was known as the 'Desert Fox'?

O Rommel

O Hess

O Donitz

49. Which Greek of the fifth century BC did the writer Cicero describe as 'the father of history'?

O Aristophanes

O Euripides

O Herodotus

50. Which quintessentially British dish was one of the few things not to be affected by rationing during the Second World War?

O Bacon and Eggs

O Fish and Chips

O Roast Beef

51. What medal was awarded to US soldiers injured in action during the Vietnam War?

O Blue Heart

O Red Heart

O Purple Heart

52. By what name is the historical figure Vladimir Ilyich Ulyanov better known?

O Stalin

O Lenin

O Trotsky

53. The early kings of which country were buried on the isle of Iona?

O Scotland

O Wales

O Ireland

54. Which fading empire became known as the 'Sick Man of Europe' in the nineteenth century?

O Mayan

O Minoan

O Ottoman

55. Which British industry found its operations reduced by a quarter after Dr Beeching's controversial and highly unnecessary 1963 report?

O Railways

O Mining

O Tourism

56. In 1415, which English king defeated the French at the Battle of Agincourt?

O Edward I

O Henry V

O George II

57. According to the legend, which creature inspired Robert the Bruce to 'try, try again', after a defeat by the English?

O Spider

O Sparrow

O Stoat

58. Enver Hoxha was the leader of which European country for over forty years until his death in 1985?

O Macedonia

O Romania

O Albania

59. What was the nickname of Bernstein and Woodward's secret contact in their Watergate investigation?

O Deep Well

O Deep Throat

O Deep Thought

60. What was the Roman name for Wales?

- *O* Hibernia
- *O* Caledonia
- *O* Cambria

61. Who was the scandalous third wife of the emperor Claudius?

- *O* Messalina
- *O* Poppaea
- *O* Agrippina

62. Which Mediterranean island was awarded the George Cross in recognition of its inhabitants' bravery during the Second World War?

- *O* Sicily
- *O* Crete
- *O* Malta

63. The site of the 1815 Battle of Waterloo is in which modern European country?

- *O* Italy
- *O* Belgium
- *O* France

64. Which English king was nicknamed 'Longshanks'?

- *O* Edward I
- *O* William II
- *O* Stephen

65. What was the name of the British Ocean liner that was controversially sunk by a German submarine on 7 May 1915?

- *O* *Titanic*
- *O* *Queen Mary*
- *O* *Lusitania*

66. 'England expects every man to do his duty', is a message given to his men by which famous leader in October 1805?

- O Wellington
- O Nelson
- O Cochrane

67. In which month is VE Day celebrated in the UK?

- O May
- O June
- O July

68. Knossos was the principal city of which ancient civilization?

- O Minoan
- O Phoenician
- O Carthaginian

69. King George III of England is thought to have suffered from which condition?

- O Porphyria
- O Autism
- O Schizophrenia

70. By 1913, which British port had become the largest exporter of coal in the world?

- O Liverpool
- O Plymouth
- O Cardiff

71. What was the first name of the US president Eisenhower?

- O Dwight
- O Deke
- O Delbert

72. General Charles George Gordon died in which African city?

- O Khartoum
- O Cairo
- O Cape Town

73. Greaves were pieces of armour worn by medieval knights to protect which part of the body?

- O Hands
- O Legs
- O Ears

74. Mary Seacole was a pioneering figure in which field?

- O Nursing
- O Architecture
- O Garden design

75. The Charge of the Light Brigade was a disastrous military action in which war?

- O Boer War
- O Crimean War
- O Peninsular War

76. Who founded the city of Bucephala, naming it after his dead horse?

- O Alexander the Great
- O Julius Caesar
- O Hannibal

77. What was the first name of the British soldier Field Marshal Montgomery?

- O Bernard
- O Jeffrey
- O Oscar

78. To which battle was Winston Churchill referring when he said, 'Never in the field of human conflict was so much owed by so many to so few'?

- O Battle of El Alamein
- O Battle of the Bulge
- O Battle of Britain

79. What name was given to the group of craftsmen, first formed in 1811, who destroyed textile machinery as they feared it would make their skills redundant?

- O Levellers
- O Chartists
- O Luddites

80. The HMS *Bounty*, famous for its mutinous sailors, was transporting saplings of which tree on its fateful journey of 1789?

- O Breadfruit
- O Coconut palms
- O Douglas firs

81. The notorious gangster Al Capone was finally convicted of which crime in 1931?

- O Forgery
- O Murder
- O Tax evasion

82. Which Roman emperor, born in AD161, believed himself to be Hercules, and fought in the arena as a gladiator?

- O Claudius
- O Nero
- O Commodus

83. Between September 1941 and January 1944, the German Army laid siege to which city of the Soviet Union?

- O Moscow
- O Leningrad
- O Kiev

84. The *Mary Rose* warship was built for which English king?

- O Henry VIII
- O William the Conqueror
- O George III

85. Cyrus the Great was the ruler of which empire in the sixth century BC?

- O Mughal Empire
- O Persian Empire
- O Roman Empire

86. Who was the wife of Henry VIII at the time of his death?

- O Anne of Cleves
- O Jane Seymour
- O Catherine Parr

87. By the end of the Hundred Years' War, what was the only French city still in the possession of the English?

- O Rouen
- O Calais
- O Le Havre

88. In the seventeenth century, what was the occupation of the infamous Jack Ketch?

- O Executioner
- O Highwayman
- O Pirate

89. In 1934, which American criminal was betrayed to the authorities by 'The Lady In Red'?

- *O* Clyde Barrow
- *O* John Dillinger
- *O* Al Capone

90. Who commanded the Prussian forces against Napoleon at the Battle of Waterloo?

- *O* Blucher
- *O* Bismarck
- *O* Frederick the Great

91. What was the name of Henry VIII's brother, the first husband of Catherine of Aragon?

- *O* Alfred
- *O* James
- *O* Arthur

92. The conquistador Hernan Cortes was instrumental in the destruction of which empire?

- *O* Aztec
- *O* Incan
- *O* Mayan

93. Who was the general secretary of the Communist Party of the Soviet Union between 1964 and 1982?

- *O* Andropov
- *O* Stalin
- *O* Brezhnev

94. In which century did Robert Walpole, regarded as Britain's first prime minister, take office?

- *O* Seventeenth
- *O* Eighteenth
- *O* Nineteenth

95. Which Greek philosopher was the teacher of Alexander the Great?

- O Aristotle
- O Plato
- O Socrates

96. Which American Civil War leader earned the nickname 'Stonewall' at the first battle of Bull Run?

- O Thomas Jackson
- O Jefferson Davis
- O Robert E. Lee

97. Which Asian country pursued a policy of isolationism for 251 years until forced to open its borders by Matthew Perry's Convention of Kanagawa in 1854?

- O China
- O Japan
- O Indonesia

98. Charles the Fat, Charles the Bald and Charles the Simple are all former kings of which country?

- O Spain
- O Ireland
- O France

99. Which title, meaning 'king' was held by the rulers of the Persian empire?

- O Sheik
- O Shah
- O Sultan

100. 'All is lost! Monks! Monks! Monks!' are reputed to be the last words of which English king?

- O Edward the Confessor
- O George V
- O Henry VIII

101. The Wall Street Crash took place on 24 October of what year?

- O 1899
- O 1919
- O 1929

102. Which Russian leader worked in the Royal Navy Dockyards at Deptford in the late seventeenth century?

- O Peter the Great
- O Vlad the Impaler
- O Ivan the Terrible

103. Which British monarch was known as 'The Sailor King'?

- O Edward VII
- O George III
- O William IV

104. Six members of whose gang were murdered in the St Valentine's Day Massacre of 1929?

- O Lucky Luciano
- O Bugs Moran
- O Dutch Schultz

105. Who led the Native American forces against General Custer at the Battle of the Little Bighorn?

- O Sitting Bull
- O Geronimo
- O Black Hawk

106. Queen Victoria belonged to which royal house?

- O Tudor
- O Stuart
- O Hanover

107. By what name was the British king George VI known to his family?

- O Billy
- O Bertie
- O Bobby

108. Which philosopher was forced to commit suicide by drinking hemlock after being found guilty of the charge of 'corrupting the young'?

- O René Descartes
- O Diogenes
- O Socrates

109. In the Second World War, 'Bevin Boys' were young men of National Service age who were chosen to work in which industry rather than join the armed forces?

- O Farming
- O Fishing
- O Mining

110. Rasputin, known as 'The Mad Monk', is said to have cured the Tsar's son of which disease?

- O Smallpox
- O Haemophilia
- O Leprosy

111. Which king was replaced by Mary II and her husband William III in the 'glorious revolution' of the seventeenth century?

- O James II
- O Richard III
- O Edward V

112. In April 1882, who shot and killed the American outlaw Jesse James?

- Robert Ford
- Kid Curry
- Ike Clanton

113. The Peloponnesian War of the first century BC was fought between Sparta and which other Greek city state?

- Athens
- Macedon
- Ithaca

114. Who was the US president at the time of the botched 'Bay of Pigs' invasion of Cuba?

- John F. Kennedy
- Lyndon B. Johnson
- Richard Nixon

115. In ancient Rome, what was the 'cloaca maxima'?

- A palace
- A stadium
- A sewer

116. Which art historian, the surveyor of the Queen's pictures for over twenty-five years, was exposed as a Soviet spy in 1979?

- Anthony Blunt
- Kim Philby
- Guy Burgess

117. In which year did Alcock and Brown make their first non-stop transatlantic flight?

- 1899
- 1919
- 1929

118. In AD41, who did Claudius replace as emperor of Rome?

- O Caligula
- O Augustus
- O Marcus Aurelius

119. The revolutionary Che Guevara was born in which country?

- O Brazil
- O Argentina
- O Jamaica

120. What nickname was given to the White House administration of president John F. Kennedy?

- O Camelot
- O Lyonesse
- O Albion

121. Which English port was built on the site of the Roman city of Clausentum?

- O Plymouth
- O Southampton
- O Grimsby

122. The explorer Captain James Cook was killed by natives on which island?

- O Tasmania
- O Fiji
- O Hawaii

123. What was the name of Oliver Cromwell's son, who assumed the title of lord protector of England after his father's death?

- O Richard
- O Robert
- O Roger

124. Against which country did El Salvador wage the so-called 'Football War' of 1969?

O Honduras

O Colombia

O Belize

125. Which English king reportedly died from eating 'a surfeit of lampreys'?

O Richard II

O Henry I

O George IV

126. The Toltec empire flourished in which country between the tenth and twelfth centuries AD?

O Colombia

O Peru

O Mexico

127. In which decade was the death penalty for murder abolished in the UK?

O 1960s

O 1970s

O 1980s

128. What name was given to the 1st US Volunteer Cavalry Regiment that took part in the Spanish-American War?

O Hard Riders

O Rough Riders

O Tough Riders

129. In 1309, which French city became the official residence of the Pope?

O Lyon

O Poitiers

O Avignon

130. What was the code name of the Allied D-Day landings of 1944?

- O Overlord
- O Emperor
- O Dominator

131. What term was used to describe imperialists who made their fortunes in India before returning to Britain to invest their wealth?

- O Bandobast
- O Badmash
- O Nabob

132. In August of 1943, which US general was reprimanded for slapping shell-shocked servicemen and accusing them of cowardice?

- O Patton
- O MacArthur
- O Pershing

133. On 16 July 1945, the first ever nuclear bomb detonation occurred in which US state?

- O New Mexico
- O Arizona
- O Alaska

134. Seven out of every ten German planes shot down during the Battle of Britain were victims of which type of British aircraft?

- O Spitfire
- O Mosquito
- O Hurricane

135. What was the first name of the Soviet spy known as 'Kim' Philby?

- O Henry
- O Horace
- O Harold

136. The huge Ishtar Gate was a landmark in which ancient city?

- O Babylon
- O Carthage
- O Persepolis

137. Butch Cassidy and The Sundance Kid were eventually shot dead in which country?

- O Panama
- O Mexico
- O Bolivia

138. 'Such is life', are reputed to be the last words of which criminal?

- O Dick Turpin
- O Ned Kelly
- O Dr Crippen

139. Which notorious pirate led a cross-land expedition to sack the country of Panama in 1670?

- O Henry Morgan
- O Edward Teach
- O William Kidd

140. In 1989, the 'velvet revolution' took place in which country?

- O Czechoslovakia
- O Romania
- O Bulgaria

141. The strict disciplinarian Draco, from whom we derive the word 'draconian', was the legislator of which Greek city in the seventh century BC?

- O Sparta
- O Delphi
- O Athens

142. What was the code name of Wing Commander Yeo-Thomas, a key figure in the French resistance during the Second World War?

- O Mock Turtle
- O Mad Hatter
- O White Rabbit

143. In 1973, the so-called 'regime of the colonels' abolished the monarchy of which country?

- O Netherlands
- O Greece
- O Denmark

144. What was the original name of Francis Drake's ship the *Golden Hind*?

- O *Pelican*
- O *Puffin*
- O *Penguin*

145. The Roman palace at Fishbourne is believed to have been built for which British client king?

- O Cogidubnus
- O Verica
- O Prasutagus

146. In May 1941, which prominent Nazi secretly flew to Scotland in an attempt to broker a peace deal between Britain and Germany?

- O Heinrich Himmler
- O Joseph Goebbels
- O Rudolph Hess

147. In Ancient Rome, which type of gladiator had only a net and a trident to defend himself?

- O Retiarius
- O Samnite
- O Secutor

148. On which island was the explorer Ernest Shackleton buried in 1922?

- O South Georgia
- O Elephant Island
- O South Helena

149. Which English city was the seat of the King Canute's government?

- O Ely
- O York
- O Winchester

150. Who was the home secretary at the time of the Sidney Street Siege of 1911?

- O Neville Chamberlain
- O Winston Churchill
- O David Lloyd George

General Knowledge

1. Balsamic vinegar is traditionally made by fermenting which fruit?

- O Grapes
- O Prunes
- O Dates

2. Which plant forms the main diet of the Giant Panda?

- O Water lilies
- O Beansprouts
- O Bamboo

3. Hank is a shortened form of which Christian name?

- O Herbert
- O Henry
- O Horace

4. In the nursery rhyme 'Sing A Song Of Sixpence', what type of bird stole the maid's nose?

- O Thrush
- O Blackbird
- O Eagle

5. What type of shop traditionally has three golden balls hanging outside it?

- O Chemists
- O Pawnbrokers
- O Butchers

6. In Victorian London, the term 'pea souper' referred to which type of weather?

- O Thick smog
- O Strong winds
- O Torrential rain

7. St Patrick is often said to have driven which creatures out of Ireland?

- O Snakes
- O Spiders
- O Scorpions

8. Which county in the north of England lends its name to a famous type of hotpot?

- O Yorkshire
- O Cumbria
- O Lancashire

9. What is the proper name of the tall, furry helmets traditionally worn by members of the Grenadier Guards in the British Army?

- O Wolfskins
- O Bearskins
- O Rabbitskins

10. Which naturally occurring mineral takes its name from the Greek for 'unquenchable'?

- O Asbestos
- O Gypsum
- O Topaz

11. The famous statue of the biblical David, located in the Accademia gallery in Florence, is a work by which artist?

- O Michelangelo
- O Rodin
- O Henry Moore

12. What is the name of someone who makes their living by dealing in stolen goods?

- O Fence
- O Door
- O Screen

13. What type of food are 'portobellos'?

- O Leeks
- O Potatoes
- O Mushrooms

14. Kosher food is prepared according to the dietary laws of which religion?

- O Sikhism
- O Islam
- O Judaism

15. The TV character Lovejoy was an expert in which field?

- O Antiques
- O DIY
- O Cookery

16. Postman Pat lives and works in which fictional village?

- O Darrowdale
- O Greendale
- O Glendale

17. *West Side Story* is a musical version of which Shakespeare play?

- O *King Lear*
- O *Much Ado About Nothing*
- O *Romeo and Juliet*

18. Which American singer was known as 'The Godfather of Soul'?

- O James Brown
- O Barry White
- O Smokey Robinson

19. In cockney rhyming slang, what is a 'whistle'?

- O Suit
- O Hat
- O Pair of Shoes

20. The Shaolin monks of China are renowned for their skill in which field?

- O Winemaking
- O Martial arts
- O Singing

21. *The Hitch-Hiker's Guide to the Galaxy* is a popular book by which science fiction author?

- O Terry Pratchett
- O Philip K. Dick
- O Douglas Adams

22. In January 2003, Rebekah Wade became the first female editor of which newspaper?

- O *Sun*
- O *Guardian*
- O *Daily Mail*

23. Which hero from Greek myth was dipped in the magical river Styx as an infant in an attempt to render him invulnerable?

- O Heracles
- O Achilles
- O Perseus

24. The 'dermis' is the technical term for which part of the human body?

- O Hair
- O Skeleton
- O Skin

25. In the nursery rhyme 'Polly Put The Kettle On', who takes it off again?

- *O* Sandie
- *O* Sukey
- *O* Sylvie

26. 'And did those feet in ancient time', is the opening line of which popular hymn?

- *O* *Rock Of Ages*
- *O* *Jerusalem*
- *O* *Abide With Me*

27. The Wright Brothers' first successful powered flight took place in which year?

- *O* 1873
- *O* 1903
- *O* 1933

28. What is the official title of the entertainment staff of Pontin's holiday camps?

- *O* Redcoats
- *O* Bluecoats
- *O* Yellowcoats

29. Tucker Jenkins and Danny Kendall were characters in which TV series?

- *O* *Press Gang*
- *O* *Byker Grove*
- *O* *Grange Hill*

30. Which huntsman adversary of Bugs Bunny carried a shotgun and spoke often of his desire to kill the 'wabbit'?

- *O* Elmer Fudd
- *O* Porky Pig
- *O* Yosemite Sam

31. In the nineteenth century, the astronomers Lowell and Schiaparelli identified long channels or 'canals' on the surface of which planet?

- O Pluto
- O Mars
- O Jupiter

32. A schoolboy named William Webb-Ellis is reputedly a pioneer of which sport?

- O Football
- O Rugby Union
- O Tennis

33. When passing through United States customs in 1882, who said he had nothing to declare but his 'genius'?

- O Oscar Wilde
- O Mark Twain
- O Henry Irving

34. What name is given to someone who can speak many languages?

- O Polyphile
- O Polygon
- O Polyglot

35. Which cereal crop is used to make single malt whisky in Scotland?

- O Oats
- O Maize
- O Barley

36. Which animals take their name from the Greek for 'double life'?

- O Amphibian
- O Reptile
- O Marsupial

37. Which symbol from British folklore, symbolizing fertility and rebirth, is also a popular pub name in the UK?

- O Red Lion
- O Green Man
- O Black Horse

38. What is the literal meaning of the Greek word 'eureka'?

- O Praise be
- O I have found it
- O Out of my way!

39. An 'orrery' is a clockwork model that demonstrates the movements of what?

- O Tides
- O Planets
- O Bowels

40. In astronomy, what are 'white dwarfs' and 'red giants'?

- O Planets
- O Comets
- O Stars

41. John Maynard Keynes was an eminent figure in which field in the twentieth century?

- O Economics
- O Architecture
- O Archaeology

42. In the Republic of Ireland, what is the Garda?

- O Parliament
- O Police force
- O National lottery

43. **The colour of a flamingo's plumage is determined by what factor?**

- O Size
- O Temperature
- O Diet

44. **What is the name of the traditional British dessert of breadcrumbs, egg whites, jam and meringue?**

- O King of Puddings
- O Prince of Puddings
- O Queen of Puddings

45. **The woman's name Ruth is derived from a Hebrew word meaning what?**

- O Truth
- O Compassion
- O Victory

46. **Which part of an egg is known as the albumen?**

- O The white
- O The yolk
- O The shell

47. **What is traditionally bought at Billingsgate Market?**

- O Flowers
- O Furniture
- O Fish

48. **Clarice Cliff is famous for designing which items?**

- O Dresses
- O Pottery
- O Ocean liners

49. Which philosophical movement, taking its name from the Latin for 'nothing', supports the theory that life has no intrinsic meaning or value?

O Nihilism

O Epicurianism

O Stoicism

50. Which highly dangerous Japanese delicacy consists of pufferfish with the poisonous sections removed?

O Rumaki

O Fugu

O Sekihan

51. Lenny Bruce was a controversial figure in which field in the 1960s?

O Cinema

O Stand-up comedy

O Stage musicals

52. 'Round up the usual suspects', is a much-quoted line from which 1942 film?

O *Casablanca*

O *Gone with the Wind*

O *Citizen Kane*

53. What is the scientific name for a female donkey?

O Jilly

O Jenny

O Jacky

54. Which flowering plant is known as the 'Sword Lily'?

O Gladiolus

O Dahlia

O Carnation

55. In the James Bond books of Ian Fleming, Ernst Stavro Blofeld was the head of which sinister organization?

- O DRAX
- O LARGO
- O SPECTRE

56. What is added to Irish stout to make the drink called a Black Velvet?

- O Whisky
- O Lager
- O Champagne

57. Which African country has a flag that is entirely green with no design or insignia at all?

- O Uganda
- O Libya
- O Morocco

58. Baron Samedi is an important figure to the followers of which religion?

- O Voodoo
- O Sikhism
- O Shinto

59. In Middle Eastern mythology, what type of creature is the 'roc'?

- O Giant snake
- O Giant lion
- O Giant bird

60. In 1985, the Greenpeace ship called the *Rainbow Warrior* was sunk by agents of which European country?

- O Germany
- O Italy
- O France

61. Until its recent name change, Tiger Bay was a dockland area in which British city?

- London
- Liverpool
- Cardiff

62. Which two comedians created the X-rated *Derek and Clive* albums in the 1970s?

- Peter Cook and Dudley Moore
- Morecambe and Wise
- Cannon and Ball

63. Which three-time World Champion darts player is nicknamed 'Old Stoneface'?

- Bob Anderson
- John Lowe
- John Part

64. 'Nine Million Bicycles' was a hit single for which singer in 2005?

- Katie Melua
- Joss Stone
- Lily Allen

65. What is the meaning of the Latin word 'ergo'?

- Lastly
- And so on
- Therefore

66. In which country does a traditional sauna experience involve rolling naked in the snow and being beaten by birch twigs?

- Japan
- Germany
- Finland

67. Which singer was formerly a cavalry officer who guarded the coffin of the Queen Mother at her funeral?

- O James Blunt
- O Damien Rice
- O James Morrison

68. Which 'special agent' solved crimes in a radio drama series of the 1940s and 50s with the help of his friends Jock Anderson and Snowey White?

- O The Saint
- O Dick Barton
- O Dick Tracy

69. Which English town is well known for its collection of concrete cows?

- O Stevenage
- O Ipswich
- O Milton Keynes

70. What was the name of the baby elephant that infamously defecated on the *Blue Peter* studio floor in 1969?

- O Lulu
- O Lana
- O Lily

71. In the nineteenth century, ladies' dresses were given their full shape by a framework made up of the bones of which animal?

- O Horse
- O Elephant
- O Whale

72. Which composer was born in Poland in 1810, but went to Paris when he was twenty and never returned to the country of his birth?

- O Liszt
- O Chopin
- O Berlioz

73. Reese Witherspoon won a Best Actress Oscar in 2006 for her portrayal of which singer?

- O June Carter
- O Patsy Cline
- O Tammy Wynette

74. Rigsby was the central character in which TV sitcom of the 1970s?

- O *Going Straight*
- O *Mind Your Language*
- O *Rising Damp*

75. Which film actress, known for her shapely legs, was the favourite pin-up of American soldiers during the Second World War?

- O Betty Grable
- O Barbara Stanwyck
- O Veronica Lake

76. 'Now is the winter of our discontent', is a line from which Shakespeare play?

- O *Macbeth*
- O *The Winter's Tale*
- O *Richard III*

77. What form of alternative medicine takes its name from the Japanese for 'universal life energy'?

- O Acupuncture
- O Reiki
- O Shiatsu

78. What was the first name of Mr Schindler, who saved over 1,200 Jews from concentration camps in the Second World War?

- O Gerhard
- O Fritz
- O Oskar

79. The traditional country practice of 'coursing' means to hunt which animal with dogs using sight rather than scent?

- O Boar
- O Hare
- O Fox

80. Which England cricket captain had a well-publicized row with the umpire Shakoor Rana in 1987?

- O Mike Gatting
- O David Gower
- O Graham Gooch

81. 'Total Eclipse Of The Heart' was a hit single for which singer in 1983?

- O Elkie Brooks
- O Kiki Dee
- O Bonnie Tyler

82. Which British athlete was famously led across the line by his father after pulling a hamstring and bursting into tears at the 1992 Olympics?

- O Derek Redmond
- O Kriss Akabusi
- O Roger Black

83. Which American folk singer had a guitar upon which was famously written 'this machine kills fascists'?

- O Pete Seeger
- O Woody Guthrie
- O Dave Van Ronk

84. What type of whale is the largest toothed animal in the world?

- O Humpback whale
- O Sperm whale
- O Killer whale

85. Which jazz musician, born in 1917, was famous for his voluminous cheeks and bent trumpet?

- O Dizzy Gillespie
- O Miles Davis
- O Chet Baker

86. What is the name of the figure of speech in which the same thing is said twice in different words?

- O Ellipsis
- O Parenthesis
- O Tautology

87. Asperger's Syndrome is thought to be a form of which other condition?

- O Autism
- O Alzheimer's
- O Arthritis

88. The fashion designer Ozwald Boateng is best known for making what sort of clothes?

- O Suits
- O Wedding dresses
- O Hats

89. Which actress met a grisly end in the shower during Alfred Hitchcock's 1960 film *Psycho*?

- O Tippi Hedren
- O Eva Marie Saint
- O Janet Leigh

90. Which goddess from Greek mythology was the counterpart of the Roman Venus?

- O Athena
- O Aphrodite
- O Hera

91. If someone is 'krumping', what are they doing?

- O Dancing
- O Sleeping
- O Fighting

92. Who played the title role in the 1980s TV series *The Singing Detective*?

- O Ben Kingsley
- O Alec Guinness
- O Michael Gambon

93. Which John Steinbeck novel depicts the journey of the Joad family from the Oklahoma Dustbowl to California?

- O *Cannery Row*
- O *The Grapes of Wrath*
- O *East of Eden*

94. The Greek billionaire Aristotle Onassis made his fortune in which industry?

- *O* Shipping
- *O* Banking
- *O* Telecommunications

95. What is the first name of Agatha Christie's sleuth Miss Marple?

- *O* June
- *O* Jean
- *O* Jane

96. Which singer, born in 1935, was nicknamed 'The Killer'?

- *O* Jerry Lee Lewis
- *O* Little Richard
- *O* Buddy Holly

97. The celebrated actor Omar Sharif is one of the world's leading players of which game?

- *O* Bridge
- *O* Backgammon
- *O* Baccarat

98. Which actress played the role of Ava Gardner in the 2004 film *The Aviator*?

- *O* Kate Beckinsale
- *O* Cate Blanchett
- *O* Kate Winslet

99. In terms of martial arts, what is the 'dojo'?

- *O* Scoring system
- *O* Roundhouse kick
- *O* Training hall

100. What sort of creatures are normally kept in a terrarium?

O Reptiles

O Fish

O Birds

101. Who wrote the influential 1957 stream-of-consciousness novel entitled *On the Road*?

O Norman Mailer

O Jack Kerouac

O Charles Bukowski

102. What was the first name of Mr Colt, the inventor of the Colt revolver?

O Samuel

O Steven

O Sidney

103. 'Last night I dreamt I went to Manderley again', is the opening line of which 1938 novel?

O *1984*

O *Rebecca*

O *The Great Gatsby*

104. Who played the role of Genghis Khan in the 1956 film *The Conqueror*?

O James Stewart

O Robert Mitchum

O John Wayne

105. In Greek mythology, which king of Lydia was forced to spend eternity in the underworld with fruit and water just out of his reach as punishment for his crimes?

O Sisyphus

O Tantalus

O Midas

106. A hendecagon has how many sides?

- O Nine
- O Ten
- O Eleven

107. What is the literal meaning of the word 'dinosaur'?

- O Terrifying lizard
- O King snake
- O Walking world

108. Tom Brokaw, Dan Rather and Peter Jennings were all famous on US television in which role?

- O Chat show host
- O Newsreader
- O Talent show panellist

109. *The Naked Ape* and *The Human Zoo* are works by which celebrated scientist and author?

- O Julian Huxley
- O Desmond Morris
- O Stephen Hawking

110. Ronnie Scott's in London is a club specializing in what type of music?

- O Jazz
- O Rock
- O Funk

111. 'I've Got You Under My Skin' and 'I Get A Kick Out Of You' are songs written by whom?

- O Cole Porter
- O Irving Berlin
- O Oscar Hammerstein

112. 'The Great Game' is a term used to describe Britain's struggle with which other nation for control of central Asia?

- O Turkey
- O Russia
- O France

113. The Gorbals is a historic area in which British city?

- O Glasgow
- O Swansea
- O Belfast

114. Which American city, the largest in the state of Michigan, has often been referred to as the 'murder capital of America' due to its high crime rate?

- O Milwaukee
- O Chicago
- O Detroit

115. In Greek mythology, what was the name of the Greek herald who was reputed to have a voice louder than that of fifty men combined?

- O Stentor
- O Argus
- O Tiresias

116. In pre-decimal currency, what coin was referred to as a 'bob'?

- O Sixpence
- O Shilling
- O Farthing

117. In 1954, who became the first person to play James Bond onscreen in a US TV adaptation of *Casino Royale*?

- O Barry Nelson
- O Steve Reeves
- O Jack Lord

118. What is the name of the groundhog that emerges from his home at Gobbler's Knob in Punxsatawney on 2 February every year to predict the length of winter?

- O Bob
- O Phil
- O Jeff

119. Which Spanish city is particularly known for the architecture of Antonio Gaudi?

- O Madrid
- O Valencia
- O Barcelona

120. In Greek mythology, who was the faithful wife of Odysseus?

- O Penelope
- O Clytemnestra
- O Megaera

121. In the Paddington books by Michael Bond, what is the name of Paddington's aunt who sent him to London bearing a note which read, 'Please look after this bear'?

- O Aunt Lucy
- O Aunt Janice
- O Aunt Sarah

122. *Quadrophenia* is a 1970s concept album by which group?

- O ELO
- O The Who
- O The Small Faces

123. Which word, meaning 'nonsense' or 'empty talk', is derived from Dutch dialect for 'soft dung'?

- O Balderdash
- O Piffle
- O Poppycock

124. Which actor played the Green Cross Code Man on television in the 1970s?

- O David Prowse
- O Peter Mayhew
- O Richard Kiel

125. Who, at the age of sixty-nine, was the oldest man to take office as president of the United States?

- O George H. W. Bush
- O Harry S. Truman
- O Ronald Reagan

126. What is Cauldron Snout on the river Tees?

- O A waterfall
- O A whirlpool
- O An island

127. The word 'negus' is a title applied to the historical rulers of which country?

- O Tunisia
- O Ethiopia
- O Kenya

128. Which politician and author won the 1953 Nobel Prize for Literature?

- O Winston Churchill
- O Harold Macmillan
- O Clement Attlee

129. Which architect designed the Millennium Dome?

- O Richard Rogers
- O Norman Foster
- O Daphne Dean

130. In the game of cricket, what name is given to the practice of verbally abusing the opposition?

- O Skiing
- O Sledging
- O Skating

131. What is a Polish 'Rum Baba'?

- O Draught horse
- O Dance
- O Sponge pudding

132. From which language do we derive the word 'dungarees'?

- O Hindi
- O Farsi
- O Norse

133. Which British athlete was criticized for whistling along to the national anthem after receiving his Olympic gold medal in 1984?

- O Sebastian Coe
- O Daley Thompson
- O Steve Ovett

134. *Memoirs of a Professional Cad* is the autobiography of which actor?

- O George Sanders
- O Errol Flynn
- O David Niven

135. What was the name of the plans proposed in 1947 to reconstruct Europe in the wake of the Second World War?

- O Marshall Plan
- O Yarwood plan
- O Turbervill Plan

136. What is the name of the Heston Blumenthal establishment, located in the village of Bray, that was voted the World's Best Restaurant in 2005?

- O The Fat Duck
- O The Fat Goose
- O The Fat Heron

137. Which gymnast holds the record for the most number of Olympic medals won in a career?

- O Olga Korbut
- O Nadia Comaneci
- O Larissa Latynina

138. Mohandas K. Gandhi studied Law at which British university?

- O London University
- O Bristol University
- O Edinburgh University

139. Which actress was memorably painted gold in the 1964 James Bond film *Goldfinger*?

- O Shirley Eaton
- O Maude Adams
- O Britt Ekland

140. The Satsuma Peninsula is a feature of which country?

- O Thailand
- O China
- O Japan

141. The Tuileries Gardens are located next to which Parisian tourist attraction?

- O The Louvre
- O The Eiffel Tower
- O The Pompidou Centre

142. Which English city became the height of eighteenth-century fashion under the influence of the celebrated dandy Beau Nash?

- O Bath
- O Birmingham
- O Norwich

143. In the obsolete tripartite system of education, children were sent either to a grammar school, a secondary modern school or what other type of establishment?

- O Farming college
- O Art school
- O Technical school

144. On a ship, what are the 'bowers'?

- O Anchors
- O Masts
- O Compasses

145. Govan is a suburb of which British city?

- O Edinburgh
- O Glasgow
- O Cardiff

146. Who was the first footballer to win 100 caps for the England national team?

- O Billy Wright
- O Stanley Matthews
- O Bobby Charlton

147. The film *Brokeback Mountain* was based on a short story by which writer?

- O Nicholas Evans
- O Larry McMurtry
- O Annie Proulx

148. Which English playwright, born in 1579, is rumoured to have co-authored *Henry VIII*, *Cardenio* and *Two Noble Kinsmen* in collaboration with William Shakespeare?

- O John Fletcher
- O Christopher Marlowe
- O Thomas Kyd

149. What was the name of Martin Luther King's wife, herself an important civil rights activist?

- O Claudia
- O Coretta
- O Calpurnia

150. What is the name of the organized crime organization that operates out of the city of Naples?

- O Camorra
- O Cosa Nostra
- O Sacra Corona

C. J. DE MOOI
Politics

Full name:
Connagh Joseph de Mooi

Home town:
Born in Barnsley, C. J. now lives in Caldicot.

Education:
Degree in English Literature and Performance Arts from St Mary's.

Quizzing credentials:

2000 Winner of *15–1.*

2000 Contestant on *The Weakest Link*. C. J. was voted off in the first round and was the first person to say anything rude about the people who had voted him off. He was invited back to take part in the *Bad Losers Christmas Special*, which he won.

2002 Winner on five shows of *100%.*

2003 Winner on *Beat the Nation.*

Strongest Eggheads subject:
Politics

Least favourite subject:
Food and Drink

Special interest:
US History

Hobbies:
Chess, TV comedy (*Frasier, Have I Got News for You* and *The Simpsons*). In fact, C. J. thinks everything he knows he learned from *The Simpsons.*

Politics

1. In which country was the politician Neil Kinnock born?

- O Wales
- O Scotland
- O England

2. Mohandas Karamchand were the first names of which leading political figure who died in 1947?

- O Gandhi
- O Ataturk
- O Nehru

3. Which politician was voted The Greatest Briton of All Time in a 2002 BBC poll?

- O Margaret Thatcher
- O Duke of Wellington
- O Winston Churchill

4. Who became vice president of the United States in 2001?

- O Colin Powell
- O Condoleezza Rice
- O Dick Cheney

5. Who made the infamous 'Rivers of Blood' speech on 20 April 1968?

- O Oswald Mosley
- O Enoch Powell
- O Kenneth Baker

6. The US president John F. Kennedy had a celebrated affair with which film star?

- O Marilyn Monroe
- O Jayne Mansfield
- O Kim Novak

7. In 1990, which MP famously fed a burger to his daughter Cordelia in order to emphasize the safety of British beef?

O Neil Hamilton

O Norman Lamont

O John Gummer

8. The 1997 Earth Summit was held in which city?

O Helsinki

O London

O Kyoto

9. Who famously said, 'It's time to get back to basics' in 1993?

O David Owen

O John Major

O Tony Blair

10. Which politician was ridiculed by the left wing for launching what has been described as a 'Hug a Hoodie' campaign in July 2006?

O David Cameron

O Jack Straw

O Oliver Letwin

11. Who became the secretary general of the United Nations in 1997?

O Kofi Annan

O Boutros Boutros-Ghali

O Javier Perez de Cuellar

12. In British politics, one full term of office for a prime minister lasts how many years?

O Three

O Five

O Seven

13. 'Would you buy a used car from this man?' was a slogan used to undermine the popularity of which US politician?

- Richard Nixon
- David Lloyd George
- Tony Blair

14. Which US president was sometimes referred to as 'The Gipper'?

- Lyndon B. Johnson
- Ronald Reagan
- Gerald Ford

15. By convention, general elections in the UK have usually been held on which day of the week?

- Saturday
- Tuesday
- Thursday

16. Who succeeded John Major as leader of the Conservative Party?

- Kenneth Clarke
- William Hague
- Iain Duncan Smith

17. In 1969, which American senator drove his car off a bridge on Chappaquiddick Island?

- Joseph McCarthy
- Gary Hart
- Edward Kennedy

18. What is the first name of George W. Bush's wife?

- Laura
- Nancy
- Hillary

19. During the run-up to the 2001 general election, which politician punched a man for throwing an egg at him?

- O Jack Straw
- O John Prescott
- O Peter Mandelson

20. Which man, MP for Rochdale between 1972 and 1992, is thought to be the heaviest Member of Parliament of all time?

- O Wentworth Schofield
- O Jack McCann
- O Cyril Smith

21. What type of people did Harold Wilson famously refer to as, 'The Gnomes of Zurich'?

- O Chocolatiers
- O Watchmakers
- O Bankers

22. Which British politician was the president of the European Commission between 1977 and 1981?

- O Roy Hattersley
- O Roy Jenkins
- O David Steele

23. Which politician revealed in 2002 that she had been the mistress of John Major for four years in the 1980s?

- O Edwina Currie
- O Ann Widdecombe
- O Theresa May

24. Which memorable headline from the *Sun* in 1979, paraphrased Jim Callaghan's supposedly cavalier attitude to the growing industrial unrest in the UK?

- O We're Doing Fine
- O Britain Is Booming
- O Crisis? What Crisis?

25. In 2003, Arnold Schwarzenegger became the governor of which US state?

- O Florida
- O California
- O New York

26. Who led the Labour Party to a landslide victory over Winston Churchill's Tories in 1945?

- O Clement Attlee
- O Ernest Bevin
- O Stanley Baldwin

27. Tony Blair attended which school?

- O Eton College
- O Winchester
- O Fettes College

28. Emmeline Pankhurst is best known for her work in which field?

- O Female suffrage
- O Prison reform
- O Abolitionism

29. Who was the president of Cuba until he was ousted by Fidel Castro in 1959?

- O Noriega
- O Batista
- O Franco

30. In 1988, Benazir Bhutto became the first female prime minister of which country?

- O India
- O Thailand
- O Pakistan

31. Kofi Annan, the Nobel Peace Prize winner and United Nations Secretary General, was born in which African country?

- O Ghana
- O Chad
- O Egypt

32. Ariel Sharon became prime minister of which country in 2001?

- O Tunisia
- O Lebanon
- O Israel

33. In what year did the London congestion charge, designed to reduce traffic in the capital, come into effect?

- O 1999
- O 2001
- O 2003

34. Which politician told the 1981 Conservative Party Conference that his father 'didn't riot. He got on his bike and looked for work'?

- O Norman Tebbit
- O Jim Prior
- O Enoch Powell

35. What is the nickname of the Labour politician Tony Benn?

- O The Grocer
- O Tarzan
- O Wedgie

36. Which political organization was founded in 1966 by Huey Newton and Bobby Seale?

- O The Black Panthers
- O Greenpeace
- O The Monster Raving Loony Party

37. Which country was described by Winston Churchill in 1939 as, 'a riddle wrapped in a mystery inside an enigma'?

- O The Soviet Union
- O China
- O West Germany

38. In which year did two general elections last take place in the UK?

- O 1974
- O 1984
- O 1994

39. Which football team does Tony Blair claim to support?

- O Liverpool
- O Newcastle United
- O Manchester United

40. In 1963, who was selected by the Queen to replace Harold Macmillan as British prime minister?

- O Anthony Eden
- O Jim Callaghan
- O Alec Douglas-Home

41. In May 1968, a general insurrection featuring student strikes and riots broke out in which country?

- O Italy
- O France
- O Ireland

42. What colour are the leather benches in the House of Lords?

- O Red
- O Black
- O Blue

43. The European Court of Human Rights is located in which city?

- O Madrid
- O Strasbourg
- O Budapest

44. What is the real Christian name of the politician 'Paddy' Ashdown?

- O William
- O Leonard
- O Jeremy

45. Who was the British prime minister at the time of the currency decimalization of the 1970s?

- O Edward Heath
- O Harold Wilson
- O Margaret Thatcher

46. Who was the first governor general of Pakistan?

- O Jinnah
- O Ali Bogara
- O Nazimuddin

47. In the British parliamentary system, whose job is it to ensure that MPs attend votes in the House of Commons?

- O Black Rod
- O Chief Whip
- O Father of the House

48. In terms of American politics, what was the 'Watergate' building?

- O Office building
- O Congressional library
- O Federal Bank

49. What is the first name of Gordon Brown's wife?

- O Bernadette
- O Sarah
- O Amanda

50. What was the name of the movement, launched by Mao Zedong in 1966, that was designed to eliminate his political rivals?

- O Political Revolution
- O Spiritual Revolution
- O Cultural Revolution

51. Who became the first minister for Scotland following devolution in 1999?

- O Alex Salmond
- O Donald Dewar
- O Charles Kennedy

52. In 1913, which suffragette stepped in front of the king's horse at the Epsom Derby?

- O Emily Davison
- O Alva Belmont
- O Lucretia Mott

53. The 1942 'Social Insurance and Allied Services' paper is better known by what name?

- O Bevan Report
- O Beveridge Report
- O Attlee Report

54. Which famously taciturn US president was the first and only president to be born on 4 July?

- O George Washington
- O William Taft
- O Calvin Coolidge

55. The Duma is the lower parliament house of which country?

- O Greece
- O Germany
- O Russia

56. Who became the director of the CIA on 30 January 1976?

- O George H. W. Bush
- O Bill Clinton
- O Donald Rumsfeld

57. Which Conservative leader once boasted to the press of his ability to drink fourteen pints of bitter in a day?

- O Iain Duncan Smith
- O Michael Howard
- O William Hague

58. Which animal is the symbol of the Republican Party in the USA?

- O Giraffe
- O Elephant
- O Rhino

59. How old was William Pitt the Younger when he first became British prime minister in 1783?

- O Twenty-four
- O Thirty-four
- O Forty-four

60. Riots occurred in which city following the controversial arrest of Leroy Alphonse Cooper on Grandby Street in 1981?

- O Bradford
- O Liverpool
- O Glasgow

61. Which Italian football club is owned by the politician and tycoon Silvio Berlusconi?

- O AC Milan
- O Juventus
- O Napoli

62. Which country elected Angela Merkel to lead its government in 2005?

- O Sweden
- O Germany
- O Spain

63. Which building in Washington is the meeting place of the US Congress?

- O The Capitol
- O The Pentagon
- O The Lincoln Memorial

64. At what item in the Commons chamber does the prime minister stand to answer prime minister's questions?

- O The Woolsack
- O The Speaker's Chair
- O The Despatch Box

65. The traitorous Vidkun Quisling was the puppet prime minister of which country during the Second World War?

- O Norway
- O Austria
- O Hungary

66. The Limehouse Declaration, issued on 25 January 1981, effectively launched which UK political party?

- O The Green Party
- O Plaid Cymru
- O The SDP

67. In 2005, which politician unwisely said of the British, 'You can't trust people who cook as badly as that,' and, 'After Finland, it is the country with the worst food'?

- Jacques Chirac
- Silvio Berlusconi
- George W. Bush

68. Who was US president at the time of the Wall Street Crash?

- Herbert Hoover
- Calvin Coolidge
- Theodore Roosevelt

69. The gaffe-prone Dan Quayle served as vice president to which US president?

- Ronald Reagan
- Jimmy Carter
- George H. W. Bush

70. Which politician, born in 1951, resigned from the cabinet in the mid-1990s to challenge John Major for the leadership of the party?

- John Redwood
- Geoffrey Howe
- Michael Heseltine

71. In September 2006, which MP was forced to apologize to the people of Papua New Guinea after linking it in a newspaper column to 'cannibalism and chief-killing'?

- Nicholas Soames
- Boris Johnson
- Lembit Opik

72. Which instrument did Bill Clinton famously play on Arsenio Hall's talk show during the 1992 presidential campaign?

- O Guitar
- O Harmonica
- O Saxophone

73. Who was the first secretary of the Soviet Union between 1953 and 1964?

- O Brezhnev
- O Stalin
- O Khruschev

74. Which British prime minister used the slogan, 'You've never had it so good', during the 1959 general election?

- O Anthony Eden
- O Harold Wilson
- O Harold Macmillan

75. Which politician held the British 100 metres record in athletics between 1967 and 1974?

- O Jeffrey Archer
- O Menzies Campbell
- O Robert Kilroy-Silk

76. Who was the second president of the United States of America?

- O John Adams
- O George Washington
- O Thomas Jefferson

77. Augusto Pinochet became president of which country in 1973?

- O Chile
- O Portugal
- O Panama

78. What is the minimum age requirement to become a candidate for president of the United States?

- O Fifty-five
- O Forty-five
- O Thirty-five

79. During a debate in 1976, who was the Conservative MP who famously seized the mace and held it above his head in the House of Commons?

- O Michael Heseltine
- O Alan Clark
- O Norman Tebbit

80. Which Northern Irish Politician won both the 1998 Nobel Peace Prize and the 2002 Gandhi Peace Prize?

- O David Trimble
- O Ian Paisley
- O John Hume

81. Which British prime minister resigned following the Suez Crisis?

- O Anthony Eden
- O Harold Wilson
- O Alec Douglas-Home

82. Gamal Abdel Nasser was the president of which country between 1956 and 1970?

- O Egypt
- O Morocco
- O Algeria

83. Which politician said that being attacked by Geoffrey Howe was akin to being 'savaged by a dead sheep'?

- O Tony Benn
- O Denis Healey
- O Michael Foot

84. Which US president, born in 1809, was re-elected with the slogan, 'Don't swap horses in midstream'?

- O Herbert Hoover
- O Thomas Jefferson
- O Abraham Lincoln

85. Michael Manley was twice prime minister of which Caribbean country?

- O Trinidad and Tobago
- O Jamaica
- O Barbados

86. Which US president granted Richard Nixon an official pardon for his role in the Watergate Affair?

- O Gerald Ford
- O Jimmy Carter
- O Bill Clinton

87. What term is used to describe a politician of flexible convictions who changes their allegiances to whatever is the popular ideology of the day?

- O Wetback
- O Trimmer
- O Filibuster

88. What does each sitting of the House of Commons begin with?

- O Prayers
- O A song
- O A bugle call

89. In which year did Charles de Gaulle finally resign the presidency of France?

- O 1949
- O 1959
- O 1969

90. Which secretary of state for trade and industry resigned in 1983 following press revelations about his affair with Sara Keays?

O Nigel Lawson

O Leon Brittan

O Cecil Parkinson

91. What is the maximum number of MPs that can sit in the House of Commons?

O 446

O 546

O 646

92. In a speech in March 1983, Ronald Reagan famously referred to the Soviet Union as what?

O A cruel regime

O A sinister axis

O An evil empire

93. John Major became the MP for which constituency in 1983?

O Buckingham

O Huntingdon

O Waveney

94. The name of which bird is applied to people who typically hold an aggressive pro-war stance?

O Hawk

O Eagle

O Osprey

95. In 2006, what was chosen as the new logo of the Conservative Party?

O A star

O A flag

O A tree

96. In 1960, which country elected the world's first female prime minister?

- *O* Rhodesia
- *O* Ceylon
- *O* Burma

97. Which politician has the unflattering nickname 'Buff'?

- *O* Jack Straw
- *O* Geoff Hoon
- *O* Paul Murphy

98. 'Doris Karloff' is the nickname of which Tory politician?

- *O* Theresa Gorman
- *O* Edwina Currie
- *O* Ann Widdecombe

99. Which politician often declares that he 'used to be the next president of the United States of America'?

- *O* John Kerry
- *O* Ross Perot
- *O* Al Gore

100. What is the practice in chamber for television broadcasts, whereby politicians sit closely around a speaking colleague to conceal poor attendance?

- *O* Doughnutting
- *O* Clustering
- *O* Packing

101. Which Cabinet post only began during Churchill's war-time government and did not exist between 1951 and 1962, or between 1963 and 1979?

- *O* Deputy prime minister
- *O* Home secretary
- *O* Defence secretary

102. Which prime minister bestowed upon Queen Victoria the title of 'Empress of India'?

- O Gladstone
- O Palmerston
- O Disraeli

103. Who succeeded Clement Attlee as leader of the Labour Party in 1955?

- O George Lansbury
- O Hugh Gaitskell
- O Harold Wilson

104. In England, unless the home secretary sets an alternative date, local government elections must take place on the first Thursday of which month?

- O April
- O May
- O June

105. Whom did George Galloway depose to become MP for Bethnal Green and Bow at the 2005 general election?

- O Anne McKechin
- O Oona King
- O Diane Abbott

106. Which journalist has been branded the 'Scud Stud' by the *New York Post* after his reports from Baghdad during the second Gulf War received worldwide attention?

- O Rageh Omar
- O John Simpson
- O Gavin Esler

107. In the 1950s and 1960s, John Prescott spent several years performing what role in the Merchant Navy?

- O Navigator
- O Engineer
- O Steward

108. What was the name of the 1969 White Paper produced by Harold Wilson's government proposing tougher controls on trade unions?

- *O* In Place of Strife
- *O* In Place of Friction
- *O* In Place of Cruelty

109. The Althing is the parliament of which European country?

- *O* Iceland
- *O* Portugal
- *O* Belgium

110. Who resigned as deputy prime minister on 1 November 1990, citing the prime minister's policies on Europe as a reason?

- *O* Willie Whitelaw
- *O* George Brown
- *O* Geoffrey Howe

111. What was the name of the woman at the centre of the Profumo Scandal of the 1960s?

- *O* Gennifer Flowers
- *O* Christine Keeler
- *O* Paula Jones

112. In the build up to the 1952 US presidential election, Richard Nixon sought to undermine the Democratic candidate, Adlai Stevenson, by referring to him as a . . . what?

- *O* Egghead
- *O* Boffin
- *O* Geek

113. Who claimed that he had, 'climbed to the top of the greasy pole', when he became prime minister in 1868?

O Disraeli

O Gladstone

O Lord Salisbury

114. Which first lady of the USA wrote a newspaper column entitled 'My Day' for over twenty-five years?

O Eleanor Roosevelt

O Betty Ford

O Nancy Reagan

115. Which present-day socialist society was founded in 1884 as an advocate of gradual rather than revolutionary social reform and numbered amongst its early members H. G. Wells and Emmeline Pankhurst?

O The 1922 Committee

O The Fabian Society

O The Chiltern Hundreds

116. By what name is the parliament building of New Zealand popularly known?

O The Bird's Nest

O The Rabbit Warren

O The Beehive

117. Which man holds the unique distinction of being both the oldest and the youngest man ever to hold the post of US secretary of defense?

O Caspar Weinberger

O Donald Rumsfeld

O Henry Kissinger

118. Who became acting leader of the Labour Party following the death of John Smith in 1994?

- O Margaret Beckett
- O John Prescott
- O Robin Cook

119. What is the name of the lawyer and former judge who investigated Bill Clinton's involvement in the Whitewater land transactions and his role in the Monica Lewinsky affair?

- O Linda Tripp
- O Kenneth Starr
- O Warren Burger

120. Which British politician won the prestigious 1969 Sydney to Hobart sailing race in his yacht *Morning Cloud*?

- O Michael Howard
- O Malcolm Rifkind
- O Edward Heath

121. Which member of the Irish parliament is known as the 'taoiseach'?

- O President
- O Chancellor
- O Prime minister

122. Which unpopular US president was impeached by Congress for 'high crimes and misdemeanours' in the nineteenth century?

- O Ulysses S. Grant
- O John Quincy Adams
- O Andrew Jackson

123. Which Australian prime minister was removed from office in an unprecedented move by the British governor general in 1975?

- O John McEwan
- O Gough Whitlam
- O William McMahon

124. Who was invested as Lord High Chancellor of Great Britain in June 2003?

- O Derry Irvine
- O Charles Falconer
- O James Mackay

125. The political term 'Tory' is taken from the Irish for what?

- O Outlaw
- O Liar
- O Coward

126. In which year were eighteen-year-olds first able to vote in general elections in the UK?

- O 1950
- O 1960
- O 1970

127. Arrested in 1976, the Gang of Four was a group of Communist politicians in which country?

- O China
- O North Korea
- O Italy

128. Which British politician has the middle names Denzel and Xavier?

- O William Hague
- O George Galloway
- O Michael Portillo

129. Which British minister for transport introduced the breathalyser test for drunk drivers in the 1960s?

- O Barbara Castle
- O Margaret Thatcher
- O Shirley Williams

130. The Jamaican politician Marcus Garvey is believed by members of the Rastafarian religion to be the reincarnation of which man?

- O King David
- O John the Baptist
- O Samson

131. In 1918, though she never actually took her seat in Parliament, who became the first woman to be elected to the House of Commons?

- O Peggy Fenner
- O Lucy Middleton
- O Constance Markiewicz

132. What does the J stand for in the name of former FBI chief J. Edgar Hoover?

- O James
- O John
- O Julian

133. In 1968, who became the first African-American woman to be elected to Congress?

- O Shirley Chisholm
- O Condoleezza Rice
- O Gwen Moore

134. Which controversial politician was once a calypso singer named 'The Charmer'?

O Jesse Jackson

O Marcus Garvey

O Louis Farrakhan

135. At the traditional state opening of parliament, the door to the House of Commons chamber is slammed shut in the face of which official?

O Black Rod

O Lord Chancellor

O Prime Minister

136. The Teapot Dome scandal exposed corruption within the administration of which US president?

O Warren Harding

O Calvin Coolidge

O Martin Van Buren

137. In 2004, Indulis Emsis became the first member of any Green Party to become a prime minister when he took power in which European country?

O Estonia

O Serbia and Montenegro

O Latvia

138. Which England cricketer stood unsuccessfully for Parliament in 1964?

Colin Cowdrey

Peter May

Ted Dexter

139. Whom did Rudolph Giuliani succeed as mayor of New York in 1993?

O David Dinkins

O Ed Koch

O Abraham Beame

140. What was the original surname of Malcolm X?

- O Small
- O Little
- O Short

141. In the fourteenth century, the introduction of which new tax provoked the Peasant's Revolt?

- O VAT
- O Income tax
- O Poll tax

142. The word 'politics' is derived from a Greek word meaning what?

- O Citizen
- O Overlord
- O Business

143. Which town elected the football mascot H'Angus the Monkey, alias Stuart Drummond, as its mayor in May 2002?

- O Hartlepool
- O Crewe
- O Blackburn

144. Which politician once held the world record for the fastest recorded consumption of beer, downing two and a half pints in just eleven seconds?

- O Bob Hawke
- O George W. Bush
- O Cyril Smith

145. Who is the only British prime minister to have been born outside the British Isles?

- O Lord Salisbury
- O Robert Walpole
- O Andrew Bonar Law

146. Mick Jagger was romantically linked with the wife of which politician in the 1970s?

O Pierre Trudeau

O Spiro Agnew

O Henry Kissinger

147. In Canada, electoral constituencies are known by what name?

O Departements

O Ridings

O Cantons

148. Which politician featured in the video to Tracey Ullman's 1984 hit single 'My Guy'?

O Neil Kinnock

O Denis Healey

O Arthur Scargill

149. By what popular name was Lyndon B. Johnson's wife known?

O Lady Butterfly

O Lady Fox

O Lady Bird

150. Which president of the USA once said, 'I am convinced that UFOs exist because I have seen one'?

O Jimmy Carter

O Dwight Eisenhower

O Harry Truman

General Knowledge

1. Which mountain range is often referred to as the 'backbone of England'?

- O Grampians
- O Cambrians
- O Pennines

2. Which is the largest species of whale in the world?

- O Blue whale
- O Sperm whale
- O Humpback whale

3. What drink, served 'shaken not stirred', is famously favoured by James Bond?

- O Whisky Sour
- O Vodka Martini
- O Gin and Tonic

4. Alcatraz Island is located in the bay of which US city?

- O San Francisco
- O New York
- O Los Angeles

5. What is the informal term for the flag of the United States of America?

- O Old Splendour
- O Old Glory
- O Old Majesty

6. Which Latin phrase means, 'let the buyer beware'?

- O Habeas corpus
- O In media res
- O Caveat emptor

7. What did Tony Blair give to George W. Bush for his birthday in 2006?

- O A Burberry sweater
- O A gold chain
- O A shell suit

8. Kippers are traditionally made by smoking which type of fish?

- O Herring
- O Tuna
- O Snapper

9. Which singer suffered what was described as a 'wardrobe malfunction' at the 2004 Superbowl half-time show?

- O Christina Aguilera
- O Britney Spears
- O Janet Jackson

10. What is the first name of the fictional character Rambo, as played on screen by Sylvester Stallone?

- O John
- O James
- O Joseph

11. What type of creature is the Duck-billed Platypus?

- O Reptile
- O Bird
- O Mammal

12. Which author was given the prisoner number FF8282 during his time in jail and wrote the first of his three *Prison Diaries* under that name?

- O Oscar Wilde
- O Joe Orton
- O Jeffrey Archer

13. What was the title of Lily Allen's first full single release, a UK Number 1 hit in July 2006?

- O Smile
- O Grin
- O Laugh

14. What was the nickname of the German statesman Otto Von Bismarck?

- O The Steel Chancellor
- O The Iron Chancellor
- O The Granite Chancellor

15. 'Consider Yourself' and 'Boy For Sale' are songs from which musical?

- O *Chicago*
- O *My Fair Lady*
- O *Oliver!*

16. Which Asian river is most sacred to members of the Hindu religion?

- O Ganges
- O Irrawaddy
- O Yellow River

17. Central Park is a feature of which of New York's boroughs?

- O Staten Island
- O The Bronx
- O Manhattan

18. In which century did the Roman army leave Britain?

- O Fifth
- O Eighth
- O Twelfth

19. Which TV series stars John Simm as a man named Sam Tyler?

O *Life on Mars*

O *Hotel Babylon*

O *Blackpool*

20. What fictional character provided Julia Donaldson and Axel Scheffler with the title of their 1999 children's book?

O The hippomuff

O The flugelwang

O The gruffalo

21. Which of the world's birds can run the fastest?

O Emu

O Ostrich

O Albatross

22. The popular author Andy McNab is a former member of which organization?

O SAS

O RAF

O Marines

23. *The Kiss* and *The Thinker* are works by which sculptor?

O Michelangelo

O Henry Moore

O Auguste Rodin

24. Fiji and Tonga are island nations in which of the world's oceans?

O Pacific

O Atlantic

O Indian

25. Which Second World War general was known as 'Old Blood and Guts'?

- O Patton
- O Eisenhower
- O Marshall

26. Who played the title role in the 1998 film *Blade*?

- O Wesley Snipes
- O Samuel L. Jackson
- O Denzel Washington

27. Which fictional character was the invention of the writer Edgar Rice Burroughs?

- O Flash Gordon
- O Sherlock Holmes
- O Tarzan

28. Though in more recent times described as an iris, which plant was originally said to be represented in the heraldic symbol the fleur-de-lis?

- O Lilac
- O Lily
- O Gladiolus

29. Which actor and film director was arrested on charges of drink-driving in July 2006?

- O Mel Gibson
- O George Clooney
- O Tom Hanks

30. 'Diamonds Are A Girl's Best Friend' is a song from which musical?

- O *Gentlemen Prefer Blondes*
- O *Let's Make Love*
- O *Funny Face*

31. A convict named Magwitch is a character in which book by Charles Dickens?

- O *Oliver Twist*
- O *David Copperfield*
- O *Great Expectations*

32. In TV's *Minder*, how did George Cole's character Arthur Daley often refer to his wife?

- O Her Majesty
- O 'Er Indoors
- O She Who Must Be Obeyed

33. Which country's occupation and repression of Tibet caused the Dalai Lama to flee in 1959?

- O China
- O North Korea
- O Soviet Union

34. Who plays the title role in the 2006 film *Superman Returns*?

- O Paul Walker
- O Brandon Routh
- O Tobey Maguire

35. Who was named as the captain of the England football team in August 2006?

- O John Terry
- O Steven Gerrard
- O Paul Robinson

36. The gymnast Olga Korbut won three Olympic gold medals in which year?

- O 1972
- O 1984
- O 1996

37. Which actress played the lead role in the 1987 film *Dirty Dancing*?

- O Molly Ringwald
- O Jennifer Grey
- O Jamie Lee Curtis

38. The mythical golden land of Eldorado was reputedly located on which continent?

- O Africa
- O Asia
- O South America

39. What was the name of the housekeeper in the TV sitcom *Father Ted*?

- O Mrs Doyle
- O Mrs Murphy
- O Mrs Crilly

40. In the human body, the 'hallux' is better known as what?

- O The earlobe
- O The back of the knee
- O The big toe

41. A 'mufti' is a legal expert in which religion?

- O Hinduism
- O Islam
- O Judaism

42. Which actor played the title role in the 2005 film *The Forty-Year-Old Virgin*?

- O Adam Sandler
- O Will Ferrell
- O Steve Carrell

43. Who played the title role in the Steven Spielberg movie *Saving Private Ryan*?

O Matt Damon

O Ben Affleck

O Brad Pitt

44. In which country was the mountaineer Sir Edmund Hillary born?

O Australia

O Canada

O New Zealand

45. Which horned and hoofed figure from Greek mythology was the god of flocks and herds?

O Pan

O Hermes

O Apollo

46. Who was the first ever winner of *Big Brother* on UK TV?

O Craig Phillips

O Jade Goody

O Cameron Stout

47. Which word is used to describe the attempt at 'peaceful coexistence' that was a feature of relations between the USA and the Soviet Union during the 1970s?

O Attaché

O Détente

O Cordiale

48. What was the name of the character played by Mackenzie Crook in the TV sitcom *The Office*?

O Keith

O Tim

O Gareth

49. Which US astronaut served as a senator for Ohio for twenty-four years from 1975?

- O Jack Swigert
- O John Glenn
- O Neil Armstrong

50. In the dish called Devils on Horseback, what foodstuff is wrapped in bacon?

- O Dates
- O Oranges
- O Prunes

51. 'Shut that door!' was the catchphrase of which entertainer?

- O Larry Grayson
- O John Inman
- O Dick Emery

52. Which dinosaur is recognizable from the line of triangular, bony plates on its back and its spiked tail?

- O Tyrannosaurus Rex
- O Stegosaurus
- O Diplodocus

53. What was the nickname of the boxer Steve Collins?

- O The Cockney Warrior
- O The Welsh Warrior
- O The Celtic Warrior

54. Who played the title role in the Woody Allen film *Annie Hall*?

- O Mia Farrow
- O Diane Keaton
- O Mariel Hemingway

55. What relation was Mary I of England to her successor Queen Elizabeth I?

- Half-sister
- Stepmother
- Cousin

56. 'If you prick us, do we not bleed? If you tickle us, do we not laugh?', are famous lines from which Shakespeare play?

- *Othello*
- *Much Ado About Nothing*
- *The Merchant of Venice*

57. Which fashion designer created the outfits for Madonna's 1990 Blonde Ambition tour, including the now-iconic 'cone bra'?

- Matthew Williamson
- Jean-Paul Gaultier
- Karl Lagerfeld

58. Mr Rochester is the hero of which 1847 novel?

- *Jane Eyre*
- *Rebecca*
- *Pride and Prejudice*

59. The flamboyant Frenchwoman Suzanne Lenglen dominated which sport in the 1920s?

- Golf
- Athletics
- Tennis

60. The singer Donna Summer is most associated with which type of music?

- Disco
- Thrash metal
- Hip-hop

61. What was the first name of Rigsby in the 1970s TV sitcom *Rising Damp*?

- *O* Richard
- *O* Raymond
- *O* Rupert

62. What is the literal meaning of the words 'magna carta'?

- *O* Power divide
- *O* Great charter
- *O* King's obedience

63. In which year did the London Underground, the world's first subterranean metro system, officially open for business?

- *O* 1863
- *O* 1903
- *O* 1943

64. What mythological creature is the symbol of the city of Lincoln?

- *O* Orc
- *O* Goblin
- *O* Imp

65. In Anglo-Saxon Britain, what title was held by magistrates or regional representatives of the king?

- *O* Wainwright
- *O* Reeve
- *O* Fletcher

66. Which organ of the human body monitors, destroys and stores red blood cells?

- *O* Spleen
- *O* Appendix
- *O* Pancreas

67. 'You're deth-picable' is the catchphrase of which Warner Brothers cartoon character?

- O Bugs Bunny
- O Daffy Duck
- O Porky Pig

68. Which actress was Tom Cruise's first wife?

- O Mimi Rogers
- O Rebecca de Mornay
- O Kelly McGillis

69. What is the first name of the cricket umpire universally referred to as 'Dickie' Bird?

- O Henry
- O Herbert
- O Harold

70. The concertmaster or leader of an orchestra usually plays which instrument?

- O Piano
- O Violin
- O Cello

71. The madman Renfield, Jonathan Harker and his fiancée, Mina Murray, are characters in which 1897 book?

- O *Frankenstein*
- O *Dracula*
- O *Jekyll and Hyde*

72. 'I was born in a crossfire hurricane and I howled at my ma in the drivin' rain', are the opening two lines of which Rolling Stones song?

- O Jumpin' Jack Flash
- O Satisfaction
- O Honky Tonk Women

73. The Italian city of Modena is well known for the production of what?

- *O* Ricotta cheese
- *O* Balsamic vinegar
- *O* Farfalle pasta

74. The two-time Superstars Champion Brian Jacks represented Great Britain in which sport?

- *O* Swimming
- *O* Gymnastics
- *O* Judo

75. Who won an Oscar for his role in the 1970 film *Ryan's Daughter*?

- *O* Alec Guinness
- *O* John Mills
- *O* Ralph Richardson

76. Which potentially fatal disease was officially declared 'eradicated' by the World Health Organization in 1980?

- *O* Rabies
- *O* Tuberculosis
- *O* Smallpox

77. Which band had a UK hit single with 'The Leader Of The Pack' in both 1972 and 1976?

- *O* The Shangri-Las
- *O* The Ronettes
- *O* The Supremes

78. What is the nickname of the *New York Times*?

- *O* The Thunderer
- *O* The Pink One
- *O* The Grey Lady

79. In rugby union, which player puts the ball into the scrums?

- O Scrum half
- O Fly half
- O Number 8

80. Which notorious criminal lived at 10 Rillington Place, London?

- O John Christie
- O Hawley Crippen
- O John Haig

81. In William Shakespeare's *Hamlet*, what was the occupation of Yorick?

- O Apothecary
- O Gravedigger
- O Jester

82. In which country was the writer Irvine Welsh born?

- O Wales
- O Ireland
- O Scotland

83. 'Obviously' and 'It's All About You' are hit singles for which band?

- O Busted
- O McFly
- O Blue

84. In 1993, which horse 'won' the void Grand National?

- O Esha Ness
- O Grittar
- O Ben Nevis

85. Man Ray was a leading figure in which field in the twentieth century?

- *O* Ballet
- *O* Photography
- *O* Architecture

86. What name is given to the list of requirements demanded by celebrities before they appear on a TV show?

- *O* Driver
- *O* Rider
- *O* Walker

87. The American Tom Ford is a leading name in which field?

- *O* Banking
- *O* Opera
- *O* Fashion

88. Which Congressional medal is the highest military decoration awarded by the United States?

- *O* Purple Heart
- *O* Medal of Honour
- *O* Silver Star

89. Who provided the voice of Charlie in the TV series *Charlie's Angels*?

- *O* John Forsythe
- *O* James Mason
- *O* Charlton Heston

90. Until 1973, what was the name of the country of Belize?

- *O* British Honduras
- *O* British Panama
- *O* British Colombia

91. What name is given to the treacherous western coasts of Namibia, the site of many shipwrecks?

- O The Skeleton Coast
- O Coast of Ghosts
- O Coast of Despair

92. In terms of a taxi cab, what is the word 'cab' short for?

- O Cabin
- O Cabana
- O Cabriolet

93. What colour is the planet Neptune?

- O Blue
- O Red
- O Green

94. Doris Schwartz and Leroy Johnson were characters in which TV series of the 1980s?

- O *Dynasty*
- O *The A-Team*
- O *Fame*

95. 'Well, you can tell by the way I use my walk, I'm a woman's man, no time to talk', are the opening lines of which Bee Gees single?

- O Stayin' Alive
- O Night Fever
- O Jive Talkin'

96. Tennessee Williams' play *A Streetcar Named Desire* is set in which city?

- O St Louis
- O New Orleans
- O Atlanta

97. Martha Graham and Christopher Bruce are pioneers in which field?

- O Fashion
- O Sculpture
- O Dance

98. Billy Bremner was the inspirational captain of which football team in the 1960s and 1970s?

- O Leeds United
- O Manchester United
- O Newcastle United

99. What was the name of Dick Dastardly's squadron in the TV cartoon series *Dastardly and Muttley in their Flying Machines*?

- O Dragon Squadron
- O Mosquito Squadron
- O Vulture Squadron

100. In October 1812, Napoleon's Grande Armée began to retreat from which major city of the world?

- O St Petersburg
- O Moscow
- O Kiev

101. In June 2006, who was announced as the new host of *Desert Island Discs*?

- O Kirsty Young
- O Kirsty Wark
- O Gabby Logan

102. What was the first name of Inspector Morse?

- O Endeavour
- O Endurance
- O Excellence

103. What kind of business did Freddie Laker famously run between 1966 and 1982?

O Computer Firm

O Bank

O Airline

104. The Pitti Palace and the Boboli Gardens are tourist attractions in which Italian city?

O Naples

O Florence

O Rome

105. What name was given to someone placed in charge of the horses at a nineteenth-century inn?

O Ostler

O Sawyer

O Chapman

106. In Greek mythology, the goddess Hera sent two serpents to kill which legendary hero when he was a baby?

O Orpheus

O Theseus

O Heracles

107. Which philosopher, born in 1844, formulated the idea of the 'Ubermensch', or 'Superman'?

O Nietzsche

O Schopenhauer

O Marx

108. Emanuel Lasker was the world champion of what between 1894 and 1921?

O Poker

O Chess

O Bridge

109. The Utah Jazz basketball team were based in which city until 1979?

- O Los Angeles
- O Miami
- O New Orleans

110. Which poet wrote, 'No man is an island, entire of itself'?

- O John Donne
- O John Keats
- O Andrew Marvel

111. During the Middle Ages, which Spanish city was particularly famous for the manufacture of swords and fine steel?

- O Bilbao
- O Toledo
- O Seville

112. What is the meaning of the word 'Uluru', the Aboriginal name for Ayers Rock?

- O Sacred heart
- O Red temple
- O Great pebble

113. What is the name of the record company co-founded by the TV presenter, journalist and nightclub promoter Tony Wilson in 1978?

- O Rockafella Records
- O Def Jam Records
- O Factory Records

114. 'Gamp' and 'bumbershoot' are alternative names for which everyday item?

- O Umbrella
- O Handbag
- O Hair Clip

115. What is the name of the extinct Madagascan bird that is believed to have been over three metres tall and weighed close to 500 kilograms?

- O Hippo bird
- O Elephant bird
- O Rhino bird

116. In the Oscar-winning 2004 film *Sideways*, the character of Miles is particularly disparaging about what variety of wine?

- O Chardonnay
- O Merlot
- O Grenache

117. As first described by Pierre Beauchamp, there are how many classical positions in ballet?

- O One
- O Three
- O Five

118. By tradition, which birds are ringed in the annual 'Upping' ceremony on the river Thames?

- O Bitterns
- O Grey herons
- O Mute swans

119. Which US president's ability with an axe in a former job earned him the nickname 'The Rail Splitter'?

- O Abraham Lincoln
- O George Washington
- O Thomas Jefferson

120. In Greek mythology, who was eaten by his own pack of hunting dogs as a punishment for seeing the goddess Artemis bathing?

- O Sisyphus
- O Actaeon
- O Prometheus

121. The boxer Joe Calzaghe, often referred to as 'The Pride of Wales', is a world champion in which weight division?

- O Super middleweight
- O Welterweight
- O Cruiserweight

122. What is the name of the dragon in J. R. R. Tolkien's book *The Hobbit*?

- O Fafnir
- O Smaug
- O Glaurung

123. The word 'mugger' is a Hindi term for which animal?

- O Crocodile
- O Monkey
- O Tiger

124. What are traditionally kept in a humidor?

- O Tropical fish
- O Vegetables
- O Cigars

125. The 'wendigo' is a cannibalistic monster from the folklore of which people?

- O Native Americans
- O Australian Aborigines
- O New Zealand Maoris

126. Mike D, Ad-Rok and MCA are members of which musical act?

- O Run-DMC
- O G-Unit
- O Beastie Boys

127. Which gunslinger of the Old West, who shares his name with an album by Bob Dylan, was reputed to be so mean that he once killed a man for snoring?

- O John Wesley Hardin
- O Kid Curry
- O Dave Rudabaugh

128. In 2006, Monty Panesar became the first representative of which religion to play test match cricket for England?

- O Sikhism
- O Islam
- O Judaism

129. Catherine Deneuve and Marie Helvin are former wives of which photographer?

- O Terry O'Neill
- O Patrick Lichfield
- O David Bailey

130. *Down In Albion* is the 2005 début album of which band?

- O Babyshambles
- O The Libertines
- O The Killers

131. Which remarkable athlete was stripped of the two gold medals he won in the 1912 Olympic games after he was proved to have played semi-professional baseball in 1909?

- O Al Oerter
- O Jackson Schultz
- O Jim Thorpe

132. What was the name of the home movie that has famously captured the 1963 assassination of John F. Kennedy?

- O Zapruder Film
- O Santilli Film
- O Patterson-Gimlin Film

133. On 25 July 1909, who made the first aeroplane flight from France to England?

- O Charles Lindbergh
- O Louis Bleriot
- O Amelia Earhart

134. The six-tackle rule is a feature of which contact sport?

- O Gaelic football
- O Basketball
- O Rugby League

135. In which year was the Cricket World Cup first held?

- O 1975
- O 1979
- O 1983

136. In which year did the BBC first begin to transmit experimental TV images to the nation?

- O 1922
- O 1932
- O 1942

137. Which English cricketer scored a century on his test match début in March 2006?

- O Alistair Cook
- O Paul Collingwood
- O Owais Shah

138. Bernadette of Lourdes is the patron saint of which profession?

- O Shepherds
- O Fishermen
- O Chefs

139. Where was Charles Dickens born?

- O Brighton
- O Portsmouth
- O Lincoln

140. Which football club sold the teenager Theo Walcott to Arsenal in 2006?

- O Plymouth Argyle
- O Norwich City
- O Southampton

141. What was the first name of Colonel Sanders, the famous Kentuckian restaurateur?

- O Hank
- O Harland
- O Earl

142. Which shipping area is named after the founder of the Met Office?

- O Fisher
- O Dogger
- O Fitzroy

143. Which artist controversially embalmed the corpse of a vagrant named Edwin McKenzie several years before Damien Hirst's more celebrated cows and sharks?

- *O* James Ensor
- *O* Robert Lenkiewicz
- *O* Paul McCarthy

144. Which singer plays the role of ex-con Jack Fate in the 2003 film *Masked and Anonymous*?

- *O* Bob Dylan
- *O* Kris Kristofferson
- *O* Johnny Cash

145. *Black Cherry* and *Supernature* are albums by which chart act?

- *O* Scissor Sisters
- *O* Goldfrapp
- *O* Armand Van Helden

146. The sousaphone, often featured in marching bands, is a more portable version of which musical instrument?

- *O* Cor anglais
- *O* Double bass
- *O* Tuba

147. Which year saw the introduction of the first Neighbourhood Watch scheme in the UK?

- *O* 1962
- *O* 1972
- *O* 1982

148. Gordon Bennett, the man whose name is commonly used as an exclamation of surprise or anger, was a leading figure in which field in the nineteenth century?

- O Engineering
- O Journalism
- O Banking

149. The area of France known as Charentes is well known for the manufacture of which items of clothing?

- O Slippers
- O Hats
- O Overcoats

150. What part of a Roman legionary's equipment was called a 'scutum'?

- O Tunic
- O Helmet
- O Shield

ARTS & BOOKS

1 Vincent Van Gogh
2 Pop Art
3 Louis de Bernières
4 *Macbeth*
5 Holly Golightly
6 Germaine Greer
7 Damien Hirst
8 Vivaldi
9 George Bernard Shaw
10 Cho Chang
11 Holden Caulfield
12 W. E. Johns
13 *The Crucible*
14 Bayreuth
15 *Spycatcher*
16 John Buchan
17 Monet
18 Sirius Black
19 Mozart
20 Wilfred Owen
21 Manchester
22 Sculpture
23 Becky Sharp
24 Dylan Thomas
25 *La Bohème*
26 Newfoundland
27 Edgar Allan Poe
28 Boxer
29 *Journey's End*
30 Architecture
31 The Charge of the Light Brigade
32 Ruritania
33 Tchaikovsky
34 Spain
35 John Milton
36 Beethoven
37 Samuel Johnson
38 Modern art
39 Flashman
40 *Brideshead Revisited*
41 Handel
42 Forty-two
43 Jump
44 Orff
45 Elgar
46 *The Tempest*
47 Charles Dickens
48 *The Godfather*
49 Alex Garland
50 Cecil Day-Lewis
51 East Anglia
52 Robert Langdon
53 Percy Bysshe Shelley
54 Fresco
55 Monet
56 Mikhail Baryshnikov
57 Bizet
58 Jimmy Porter
59 George
60 Violin
61 Oscar Wilde
62 The Man Who Would Be King
63 *Rebecca*
64 James Thurber
65 *The Maltese Falcon*
66 Tom Stoppard
67 Hull
68 *Fidelio*
69 Cat
70 Richard
71 *Lolita*
72 Charles Dickens
73 *Glengarry Glen Ross*
74 Asperger's
75 Leslie Charteris
76 W. H. Auden
77 Arthur Hastings
78 Sauron
79 George du Maurier
80 Lady Caroline Lamb

81 Peter Carey
82 *Rigoletto*
83 Turner
84 Piano
85 Helen of Troy
86 Deafness
87 Ira Levin
88 Titian
89 Leopold
90 Jack Aubrey
91 Farce
92 Lyra
93 Rembrandt
94 Patricia Cornwell
95 Flute
96 Iago
97 The Factory
98 *1984*
99 Jackson Pollock
100 *Porgy and Bess*
101 *Treasure Island*
102 Jay
103 Budgie
104 *The Water Babies*
105 Alexander Pope
106 Elgar
107 T. S. Eliot
108 Cat
109 Robert Burns
110 Tahiti
111 Paul McCartney
112 Organ
113 Suetonius
114 Christopher Marlowe
115 *Moby-Dick*
116 Eroica
117 Arthur Conan Doyle
118 William Burroughs
119 Mike Leigh
120 Francis Bacon
121 George Bernard Shaw
122 Margate
123 *The Caretaker*
124 Dukas
125 Wagner
126 Tom Wolfe
127 Hanif Kureishi
128 Castleford
129 The Royal Philharmonic Orchestra
130 Netherlands
131 John Le Carré
132 Frank McCourt
133 Marcel Duchamp
134 Beowulf
135 Baroque
136 Patrick Marber
137 Sherlock Holmes
138 Walt Whitman
139 *The Portrait of Dr Gachet*
140 Leisure
141 *The Wasp Factory*
142 Ode to a Nightingale
143 Pamela
144 *Colonel Sun*
145 *George Crabbe*
146 Theodore Hickman
147 Jean-Paul Sartre
148 Thomas Mann
149 Calpurnia
150 Michael Nyman

GENERAL KNOWLEDGE

1 Eminem
2 Cow
3 Hats
4 Cannes
5 Japan
6 Flute
7 The Women's Institute
8 Iceland
9 Martin Luther King
10 Methuselah
11 *Citizen Kane*
12 Buddhism
13 Brian Potter
14 Uganda
15 Gerald Ratner
16 Shilpa Shetty
17 Lionel Ritchie
18 Darts
19 Shoes
20 1986
21 Wildebeest
22 Walker
23 St Mary-le-Bow
24 Rabies
25 'Who loves ya, baby?'
26 Swimming
27 *Apocalypse Now*
28 Glenn Hoddle
29 Billy the Kid
30 Port Said
31 Rolls Royce
32 Jarvis Cocker
33 1620
34 Tiger
35 January
36 Robert Maxwell
37 Manchester
38 Basil D'Oliveira
39 New Orleans
40 Michael Fish
41 Sternum
42 Nile
43 Arrows
44 Bill Shankly
45 Las Vegas
46 Sixpence
47 Banshee
48 Electrician
49 Isis
50 Six
51 Hasim Rahman
52 Charon
53 Brazil
54 Charlton Heston
55 Netherlands
56 Belarus
57 Superman
58 Billie Holiday
59 Ken Dodd
60 Ravens
61 Monaco
62 Shiatsu
63 Rio Grande
64 Ugly Rumours
65 Arkansas
66 M62
67 *Camelot*
68 Liquorice
69 Liberace
70 Sikhism
71 Mae West
72 Thomas
73 Nepal
74 South Africa
75 Yellow
76 *The Magic Roundabout*
77 Marines
78 Noisy spirit
79 Sunflower
80 Radcliffe College
81 Hoovervilles
82 The Queen
83 *On the Waterfront*
84 Suffolk
85 The Jam

86 Niccolò Machiavelli
87 David Sheppard
88 Tin
89 *The Times*
90 Newmarket
91 *The Philadelphia Story*
92 Salome
93 Knight
94 Liverpool
95 Mrs Worthington
96 Hugh Laurie
97 Charles Lindbergh
98 Switzerland
99 Paris
100 Costermonger
101 Oedipus
102 Benjamin Spock
103 Headscarf
104 Jimmy Connors
105 Ronald Searle
106 Harold Macmillan
107 Backgammon
108 Field Marshal
109 Pope
110 Hyde Park
111 John Le Mesurier
112 Goldeneye
113 Henry VI
114 René Descartes
115 Tasmania
116 Princess Anne
117 Alexander the Great
118 Caspian Sea
119 Ava Gardner
120 George Leigh Mallory
121 Bobby Riggs
122 Churchill
123 Larry Holmes
124 Leicester
125 Emil Jannings
126 *Oliver Twist*
127 Politics
128 Oxford
129 Oxymoron
130 White smoke
131 Shiva
132 *Gypsy Moth IV*
133 Nina Simone
134 Norway
135 Dior
136 Iceland
137 Potholing
138 Rhode Island
139 Duck
140 Cat's eyes
141 Thomas Edison
142 Milos Forman
143 Rudyard Kipling
144 Cribbage
145 Clematis
146 SAS
147 Bluebeard
148 George Lazenby
149 Max Hastings
150 Timothy Leary

FOOD & DRINK

1 Spain
2 Tequila
3 Prawn
4 Avocado
5 Marmalade
6 Marengo
7 Burnt cream
8 Antipasti
9 Norwich City
10 Sheep
11 Leek
12 Edwina Currie
13 Lobster
14 Germany
15 Ireland
16 Buffalo
17 Custard
18 Native Americans
19 Vodka
20 Peach
21 Peanut
22 Potatoes
23 Himalayas
24 Blanching
25 Cherry
26 Almond
27 A Greek spirit
28 Norway
29 Pavlova
30 Fish
31 Soup
32 Juniper
33 Grapes
34 Soup
35 Bread
36 Apple
37 Diane
38 Paprika
39 Chop Suey
40 Cappuccino
41 Derbyshire
42 Cornish pasty
43 Bourbon
44 Very dry
45 Earl Grey
46 Michael Winner
47 Perignon
48 Donkey
49 Wasabi
50 Basil
51 Vine leaves
52 Potato
53 Ghee
54 Italy
55 Conchiglie
56 Carbohydrate
57 Poland
58 Ham
59 Mushrooms
60 Greek
61 Caviar
62 Kahula
63 Cheese
64 Austria
65 Broad bean
66 Intestines
67 Norwich
68 California
69 Ricotta
70 Turkey
71 Omelette
72 Daiquiri
73 Hops
74 Walnuts
75 India
76 Sicily
77 Raspberry
78 Fish heads
79 Cheese
80 Apple
81 Chestnuts
82 Blackcurrant
83 Cooking pot
84 Tonic water
85 Ginger ale
86 Graham Kerr
87 Cauliflower
88 Salmon
89 Artichoke
90 Plum

91 Strudel
92 Australia
93 Paella
94 Brisket
95 Potato
96 Lemon
97 Cheese
98 Ginger
99 Jelly
100 Bath
101 Lassi
102 Manhattan
103 Oysters
104 Coffee
105 New Orleans
106 Vegetable soup
107 Soul food
108 Oyster
109 Pluck
110 Christmas
111 Parsley sauce
112 Hindi
113 Galliano
114 Sword
115 Scotch Woodcock
116 Stew
117 Dhansak
118 China
119 Tangerine
120 Port
121 Frying pan
122 Oenophile
123 Sliced bread
124 Arborio
125 Maize
126 Mushroom
127 Brazil
128 Johnny
129 Hungary
130 Rennet
131 Unleavened bread
132 Salmon
133 Cheek
134 A baked egg
135 Haricot beans
136 The heat of a chilli
137 Balthazar
138 Worcester sauce
139 Lunch
140 Quince
141 Unleavened bread
142 Table of buttered bread
143 Mock turtle soup
144 Crab meat
145 Lemon and almond tart
146 The Savoy
147 Indonesia
148 Oatcake
149 Camembert
150 Cheese

GENERAL KNOWLEDGE

1 Gretna
2 Jordan
3 June
4 Moulin Rouge
5 November
6 Shrove Tuesday
7 Charles Atlas
8 Christopher Lee
9 Arctic Monkeys
10 Swansea
11 1992
12 Candles
13 Violins
14 Shoes
15 Poland
16 Ruby
17 Rhodes
18 Seventeenth
19 Justin Timberlake
20 *The Taming of the Shrew*
21 Tombstone
22 Wales
23 Lazarus
24 Four
25 Jamelia
26 Salvation Army
27 *Oklahoma!*
28 Television
29 Kent
30 David Blaine
31 Jay-Z
32 China
33 Killer whale
34 Prime number
35 Blood
36 Scotland
37 Sheep
38 Stamp
39 Apple
40 17 March
41 Amy
42 Statue of Liberty
43 Apache
44 The Clash
45 George Mallory
46 Aintree
47 Jacket
48 Twenty-one
49 In The Bleak Midwinter
50 William Randolph Hearst
51 Colin Meads
52 *Spaced*
53 *Chicago*
54 Lawrence Oates
55 New York
56 Patrick Lichfield
57 South America
58 Imran Khan
59 European
60 East Germany
61 Wales
62 Mr McGregor
63 Howard Hughes
64 Ireland
65 Anubis
66 The Declaration of Independence
67 South America
68 *Reader's Digest*
69 Czechoslovakia
70 Monopoly
71 Doncaster
72 Andromeda
73 Clubs
74 Salzburg
75 Mah Jong
76 A dance
77 Old people
78 George W. Bush
79 Capuchin
80 Dressmaker
81 Yellowstone
82 Leeds United
83 League
84 Dagger
85 Gordonstoun
86 South Africa

87 John Lennon
88 Margaret Thatcher
89 Denmark
90 Edinburgh
91 Chelsea
92 Atlantic City
93 Cedar
94 Poland
95 Batman
96 Bob Woodward
97 Flanders and Swann
98 Journalists
99 Jim Broadbent
100 Carthage
101 Royal Navy
102 John Prescott
103 Sword
104 Ukulele
105 Menelaus
106 John Surtees
107 Teaching
108 Isle of Man
109 Rudyard Kipling
110 Table
111 Nadia Comaneci
112 David Carradine
113 Diving
114 Grandson
115 Dorset
116 Joe Swail
117 Stella McCartney
118 Edinburgh
119 Underwater
120 Red Crescent
121 Basalt
122 Hansie Cronje
123 Dennis Hopper
124 *Calvin and Hobbes*
125 Copernicus
126 Sahara
127 Jersey
128 Beatrix
129 Dragon
130 Vitamin C
131 Durham
132 Ursula
133 Richard Gere
134 Ambush
135 Vlad the Impaler
136 Sid James
137 Roger McGough
138 Barrister
139 Farmer
140 Helen Wills Moody
141 Puglia
142 Drove
143 Orwell
144 Chris Tarrant
145 Clara Bow
146 Kenya
147 Brian Fletcher
148 Mesopotamia
149 John Newcombe
150 Nine

SCIENCE

1 Cloud
2 Galaxy
3 Australia
4 Plankton
5 Lead
6 Lacrimal
7 Saturn
8 Gemini
9 Dragonfly
10 Myopia
11 Salt
12 Memory
13 One hundred
14 Carp
15 Mercury
16 Lactic
17 Volcano
18 Brass
19 Hypotenuse
20 Bees
21 Ear
22 Apple
23 Carbon
24 Seasonal
25 1967
26 Eucalyptus
27 Hippocrates
28 South America
29 Nitrogen
30 Ebola virus
31 Light
32 Cactus
33 Work
34 Thomas Edison
35 Osmosis
36 Hands
37 Alfred
38 Infinity
39 Chimpanzee
40 Earth
41 Malaria
42 Antelope
43 Insulin
44 *Sputnik-1*
45 Fish
46 Petroleum
47 Whale shark
48 Marlin
49 Insects
50 Magnesium
51 Fish
52 Calf
53 Mars
54 Butterflies
55 Willow
56 Isaac Newton
57 Barracuda
58 Throat
59 Chickenpox
60 Great auk
61 Tsetse fly
62 Bees
63 Biro
64 Pulmonary
65 Cuckoo
66 Vitamin D
67 Helen Sharman
68 Helicopter
69 Bird
70 Stockholm syndrome
71 Mantle
72 Internet
73 Neck
74 Tetanus
75 Rattlesnake
76 Edward Jenner
77 Shoulder
78 Indonesia
79 Women
80 Horse
81 Chuck Yeager
82 Ear
83 Carbon dioxide
84 Seahorse
85 Maxilla
86 Kidneys
87 Galaxy
88 Jellyfish
89 *Thrust SSC*

90 Watt
91 Orang-utan
92 Pathology
93 St Elmo's Fire
94 Panagea
95 1986
96 Bruxism
97 Polio
98 Orchid
99 Phlegm
100 Alan Shepard
101 Cow
102 Rocks
103 Platelets
104 Andes
105 Edwin
106 Sneezing
107 A flowering plant
108 Tuberculosis
109 Arabic
110 Samuel
111 Mauritius
112 Mathematics
113 Marie Curie
114 Charles Darwin
115 Twenty-three
116 Apatosaurus
117 Wind speed
118 Blushing
119 Nitrous oxide
120 Italy
121 Wanderer
122 Archimedes
123 Wormhole
124 Sedna
125 Tannic acid
126 John Glenn
127 Genetics
128 Robert Hooke
129 Heart
130 Cyril Parkinson
131 Jupiter
132 Argon
133 Meteor shower
134 Joseph Lister
135 Sirius
136 Fairy penguin
137 Marie Curie
138 Roger Bacon
139 Tuna
140 Louis Pasteur
141 King cobra
142 Pluto
143 Parrot
144 Methane
145 Formic acid
146 Silver
147 Cobalt
148 Riboflavin
149 Big Crunch
150 Peristalsis

GENERAL KNOWLEDGE

1 Children
2 Personal
3 Kelley's Eye
4 Cat
5 Manila paper
6 Tuppenny rice
7 1999
8 Ludo
9 Mexico
10 Alaska
11 Cricket
12 Poker
13 Oliver North
14 Chas and Dave
15 Thursday
16 *Hamlet*
17 1988
18 Colours
19 1950s
20 Horse chestnut
21 Dice
22 *Crackerjack*
23 The Fantastic Four
24 Photography
25 Hill
26 Birmingham
27 King Arthur
28 Carpentry
29 Waterfall
30 Horseshoes
31 Dolcelatte
32 'Enry's 'Ammer
33 Commander
34 Odysseus
35 Shoes
36 Tic-Tac-Toe
37 Snooker
38 Oysters
39 Underground railroad
40 *Robinson Crusoe*
41 Policemen
42 Stegosaurus
43 Silks
44 Alps
45 Sebastian Coe
46 Swimming
47 Bobsled
48 *Peter Pan*
49 Drums
50 Guns 'n' Roses
51 Ernie Wise
52 Hydra
53 Kevin Keegan
54 The Streets
55 Little Boy Blue
56 Tap
57 *Annie Get Your Gun*
58 Rupert the Bear
59 Boat
60 Madonna
61 Cathy Gale
62 Gordon Richards
63 Ade Edmonson
64 The Beach Boys
65 Nookie Bear
66 Mississippi
67 Dorothy Parker
68 Spencer Perceval
69 Aston Villa
70 P. T. Barnum
71 Franz Beckenbauer
72 Al Martino
73 Lon Chaney
74 Minim
75 Lard
76 Montmartre
77 Harry Houdini
78 New Zealand
79 Flash Gordon
80 Japan
81 Barry McGuigan
82 *The Apartment*
83 Kangaroos
84 The Seychelles
85 Prince Andrew
86 Netherlands

87 Daedalus
88 Theo
89 Twenty-One
90 Malcolm X
91 *Anna Karenina*
92 Sean Kerly
93 Swede
94 George C. Scott
95 *Vanilla Sky*
96 Cab Calloway
97 Dudley Moore
98 China
99 Haiti
100 Gainsborough
101 David Berkowitz
102 *The Sopranos*
103 The Ritz
104 Postcards
105 Switzerland
106 Gary Hart
107 Loganberry
108 Jerry Springer
109 Furniture
110 Judaism
111 *Just a Minute*
112 Apollo
113 Mexico
114 Fencing
115 Robert Johnson
116 *The Perishers*
117 Spear
118 Contralto
119 Oxford
120 De Havilland
121 Four
122 Fay Weldon
123 Australia
124 The Gentle Giant
125 Gene Hackman
126 Railway station
127 1978
128 Robert Mitchum
129 Bob Hoskins
130 William Blake
131 Frank Gehry
132 Houses of Parliament
133 *Daily Telegraph*
134 Chile
135 Pretzel
136 Bing Crosby
137 *The King and I*
138 Public Enemy
139 Randolph Turpin
140 Philip Larkin
141 Sceptre
142 Carwyn James
143 *Daily Courant*
144 Ordinary Bicycle
145 Finland
146 Ryan O'Neal
147 George
148 Aeschylus
149 Sheffield
150 Charles

HISTORY

1 Spartacus
2 Abraham Lincoln
3 *Hindenburg*
4 Napoleon Bonaparte
5 Vesuvius
6 Henry Morton Stanley
7 Doc Holliday
8 Ronnie Biggs
9 Alfred the Great
10 1947
11 McCarthy
12 Enigma
13 Vichy
14 Ellis Island
15 Neville Chamberlain
16 California
17 Lady Jane Grey
18 John
19 Drake
20 The Palace of Versailles
21 First World War
22 Romanov
23 Italy
24 1912
25 France
26 Samurai
27 Monaco
28 Xanadu
29 Ironsides
30 Christopher Wren
31 First World War
32 Normandy
33 American Revolution
34 Kitchener
35 USA
36 Israel
37 Argentina
38 Doodlebug
39 Windows
40 Seventeenth
41 The Alamo
42 Genghis Khan
43 Minutemen
44 Roman emperors
45 Walter Raleigh
46 Hastings
47 Coal mining
48 Rommel
49 Herodotus
50 Fish and Chips
51 Purple Heart
52 Lenin
53 Scotland
54 Ottoman
55 Railways
56 Henry V
57 Spider
58 Albania
59 Deep Throat
60 Cambria
61 Messalina
62 Malta
63 Belgium
64 Edward I
65 *Lusitania*
66 Nelson
67 May
68 Minoan
69 Porphyria
70 Cardiff
71 Dwight
72 Khartoum
73 Legs
74 Nursing
75 Crimean War
76 Alexander the Great
77 Bernard
78 Battle of Britain
79 Luddites
80 Breadfruit
81 Tax evasion
82 Commodus
83 Leningrad
84 Henry VIII

85 Persian Empire
86 Catherine Parr
87 Calais
88 Executioner
89 John Dillinger
90 Blucher
91 Arthur
92 Aztec
93 Brezhnev
94 Eighteenth
95 Aristotle
96 Thomas Jackson
97 Japan
98 France
99 Shah
100 Henry VIII
101 1929
102 Peter the Great
103 William IV
104 Bugs Moran
105 Sitting Bull
106 Hanover
107 Bertie
108 Socrates
109 Mining
110 Haemophilia
111 James II
112 Robert Ford
113 Athens
114 John F. Kennedy
115 A sewer
116 Anthony Blunt
117 1919
118 Caligula
119 Argentina
120 Camelot
121 Southampton
122 Hawaii
123 Richard
124 Honduras
125 Henry I
126 Mexico
127 1960s
128 Rough Riders
129 Avignon
130 Overlord
131 Nabob
132 Patton
133 New Mexico
134 Hurricane
135 Harold
136 Babylon
137 Bolivia
138 Ned Kelly
139 Henry Morgan
140 Czechoslovakia
141 Athens
142 White Rabbit
143 Greece
144 *Pelican*
145 Cogidubnus
146 Rudolph Hess
147 Retiarius
148 South Georgia
149 Winchester
150 Winston Churchill

GENERAL KNOWLEDGE

1 Grapes
2 Bamboo
3 Henry
4 Blackbird
5 Pawnbrokers
6 Thick smog
7 Snakes
8 Lancashire
9 Bearskins
10 Asbestos
11 Michelangelo
12 Fence
13 Mushrooms
14 Judaism
15 Antiques
16 Greendale
17 *Romeo and Juliet*
18 James Brown
19 Suit
20 Martial arts
21 Douglas Adams
22 *Sun*
23 Achilles
24 Skin
25 Sukey
26 *Jerusalem*
27 1903
28 Bluecoats
29 *Grange Hill*
30 Elmer Fudd
31 Mars
32 Rugby Union
33 Oscar Wilde
34 Polyglot
35 Barley
36 Amphibian
37 Green Man
38 I have found it
39 Planets
40 Stars
41 Economics
42 Police force
43 Diet
44 Queen of Puddings
45 Compassion
46 The white
47 Fish
48 Pottery
49 Nihilism
50 Fugu
51 Stand-up comedy
52 *Casablanca*
53 Jenny
54 Gladiolus
55 SPECTRE
56 Champagne
57 Libya
58 Voodoo
59 Giant bird
60 France
61 Cardiff
62 Peter Cook and Dudley Moore
63 John Lowe
64 Katie Melua
65 Therefore
66 Finland
67 James Blunt
68 Dick Barton
69 Milton Keynes
70 Lulu
71 Whale
72 Chopin
73 June Carter
74 *Rising Damp*
75 Betty Grable
76 *Richard III*
77 Reiki
78 Oskar
79 Hare
80 Mike Gatting
81 Bonnie Tyler
82 Derek Redmond
83 Woody Guthrie
84 Sperm whale
85 Dizzy Gillespie
86 Tautology
87 Autism
88 Suits

89 Janet Leigh
90 Aphrodite
91 Dancing
92 Michael Gambon
93 *The Grapes of Wrath*
94 Shipping
95 Jane
96 Jerry Lee Lewis
97 Bridge
98 Kate Beckinsale
99 Training hall
100 Reptiles
101 Jack Kerouac
102 Samuel
103 *Rebecca*
104 John Wayne
105 Tantalus
106 Eleven
107 Terrifying lizard
108 Newsreader
109 Desmond Morris
110 Jazz
111 Cole Porter
112 Russia
113 Glasgow
114 Detroit
115 Stentor
116 Shilling
117 Barry Nelson
118 Phil
119 Barcelona
120 Penelope
121 Aunt Lucy
122 The Who
123 Poppycock
124 David Prowse
125 Ronald Regan
126 A waterfall
127 Ethiopia
128 Winston Churchill
129 Norman Foster
130 Sledging
131 Sponge pudding
132 Hindi
133 Daley Thompson
134 George Sanders
135 Marshall Plan
136 The Fat Duck
137 Larissa Latynina
138 London University
139 Shirley Eaton
140 Japan
141 The Louvre
142 Bath
143 Technical school
144 Anchors
145 Glasgow
146 Billy Wright
147 Annie Proulx
148 John Fletcher
149 Coretta
150 Camorra

POLITICS

1 Wales
2 Gandhi
3 Winston Churchill
4 Dick Cheney
5 Enoch Powell
6 Marilyn Monroe
7 John Gummer
8 Kyoto
9 John Major
10 David Cameron
11 Kofi Annan
12 Five
13 Richard Nixon
14 Ronald Reagan
15 Thursday
16 William Hague
17 Edward Kennedy
18 Laura
19 John Prescott
20 Cyril Smith
21 Bankers
22 Roy Jenkins
23 Edwina Currie
24 Crisis? What Crisis?
25 California
26 Clement Attlee
27 Fettes College
28 Female suffrage
29 Batista
30 Pakistan
31 Ghana
32 Israel
33 2003
34 Norman Tebbit
35 Wedgie
36 The Black Panthers
37 The Soviet Union
38 1974
39 Newcastle United
40 Alec Douglas-Home
41 France
42 Red
43 Strasbourg
44 Jeremy
45 Edward Heath
46 Jinnah
47 Chief Whip
48 Office building
49 Sarah
50 Cultural Revolution
51 Donald Dewar
52 Emily Davison
53 Beveridge Report
54 Calvin Coolidge
55 Russia
56 George H. W. Bush
57 William Hague
58 Elephant
59 Twenty-four
60 Liverpool
61 AC Milan
62 Germany
63 The Capitol
64 The Despatch Box
65 Norway
66 The SDP
67 Jacques Chirac
68 Herbert Hoover
69 George H. W. Bush
70 John Redwood
71 Boris Johnson
72 Saxophone
73 Krushchev
74 Harold Macmillan
75 Menzies Campbell
76 John Adams
77 Chile
78 Thirty-five
79 Michael Heseltine
80 John Hume
81 Anthony Eden

82 Egypt
83 Denis Healey
84 Abraham Lincoln
85 Jamaica
86 Gerald Ford
87 Trimmer
88 Prayers
89 1969
90 Cecil Parkinson
91 646
92 A cruel regime
93 Huntingdon
94 Hawk
95 A tree
96 Ceylon
97 Geoff Hoon
98 Ann Widdecombe
99 Al Gore
100 Doughnutting
101 Deputy prime minister
102 Disraeli
103 Hugh Gaitskell
104 May
105 Oona King
106 Rageh Omar
107 Steward
108 In Place of Strife
109 Iceland
110 Geoffrey Howe
111 Christine Keeler
112 Egghead
113 Disraeli
114 Eleanor Roosevelt
115 The Fabian Society
116 The Beehive
117 Donald Rumsfeld
118 Margaret Beckett
119 Kenneth Starr
120 Edward Heath
121 Prime minister
122 Andrew Jackson
123 Gough Whitlam
124 Charles Falconer
125 Outlaw
126 1970
127 China
128 Michael Portillo
129 Barbara Castle
130 John the Baptist
131 Constance Markiewicz
132 John
133 Shirley Chisholm
134 Louis Farrakhan
135 Black Rod
136 Warren Harding
137 Latvia
138 Ted Dexter
139 David Dinkins
140 Little
141 Poll tax
142 Citizen
143 Hartlepool
144 Bob Hawke
145 Andrew Bonar Law
146 Pierre Trudeau
147 Ridings
148 Neil Kinnock
149 Lady Bird
150 Jimmy Carter

GENERAL KNOWLEDGE

1 Pennines
2 Blue whale
3 Vodka Martini
4 San Francisco
5 Old Glory
6 Caveat emptor
7 A Burberry sweater
8 Herring
9 Janet Jackson
10 John
11 Mammal
12 Jeffrey Archer
13 Smile
14 The Iron Chancellor
15 *Oliver!*
16 Ganges
17 Manhattan
18 Fifth
19 *Life On Mars*
20 The gruffalo
21 Ostrich
22 SAS
23 Auguste Rodin
24 Pacific
25 Patton
26 Wesley Snipes
27 Tarzan
28 Lily
29 Mel Gibson
30 *Gentlemen Prefer Blondes*
31 *Great Expectations*
32 'Er Indoors
33 China
34 Brandon Routh
35 John Terry
36 1972
37 Jennifer Grey
38 South America
39 Mrs Doyle
40 The big toe
41 Islam
42 Steve Carrell
43 Matt Damon
44 New Zealand
45 Pan
46 Craig Phillips
47 Détente
48 Gareth
49 John Glenn
50 Prunes
51 Larry Grayson
52 Stegosaurus
53 The Celtic Warrior
54 Diane Keaton
55 Half-sister
56 *The Merchant of Venice*
57 Jean-Paul Gaultier
58 *Jane Eyre*
59 Tennis
60 Disco
61 Rupert
62 Great charter
63 1863
64 Imp
65 Reeve
66 Spleen
67 Daffy Duck
68 Mimi Rogers
69 Harold
70 Violin
71 *Dracula*
72 Jumpin' Jack Flash
73 Balsamic vinegar
74 Judo
75 John Mills
76 Smallpox
77 The Shangri-Las
78 The Grey Lady
79 Scrum half
80 John Christie
81 Jester
82 Scotland
83 McFly
84 Esha Ness

85 Photography
86 Rider
87 Fashion
88 Medal of Honour
89 John Forsythe
90 British Honduras
91 The Skeleton Coast
92 Cabriolet
93 Blue
94 *Fame*
95 Stayin' Alive
96 New Orleans
97 Dance
98 Leeds United
99 Vulture Squadron
100 Moscow
101 Kirsty Young
102 Endeavour
103 Airline
104 Florence
105 Ostler
106 Heracles
107 Nietzsche
108 Chess
109 New Orleans
110 John Donne
111 Toledo
112 Great pebble
113 Factory Records
114 Umbrella
115 Elephant bird
116 Merlot
117 Five
118 Mute swans
119 Abraham Lincoln
120 Actaeon
121 Super middleweight
122 Smaug
123 Crocodile
124 Cigars
125 Native Americans
126 Beastie Boys
127 John Wesley Hardin
128 Sikhism
129 David Bailey
130 Babyshambles
131 Jim Thorpe
132 Zapruder Film
133 Louis Bleriot
134 Rugby League
135 1975
136 1932
137 Alistair Cook
138 Shepherds
139 Portsmouth
140 Southampton
141 Harland
142 Fitzroy
143 Robert Lenkiewicz
144 Bob Dylan
145 Goldfrapp
146 Tuba
147 1982
148 Journalism
149 Slippers
150 Shield